DISCLAIMER

This book is for educational and information purposes only and is not intended as mental health treatment. Should you learn through the information shared here that treatment is indicated, contact a licensed therapist in your state. If you are having a mental health emergency, call 911, go to your nearest emergency room, or call the Military Crisis Line at 1-800-273-8255.

The National Suicide Prevention Hotline can be reached by phone at 1-800-273-TALK (1-800-273-8255) or TTY: 1-800-799-4889. This hotline is a 24-hour, toll-free suicide prevention service available to anyone in suicidal crisis. You will be routed to the closest possible crisis center in your area. Your call is free and confidential.

The Veterans Crisis Line provides confidential help through chat (www.veteranscrisisline.net/get-help/chat) and text at 838255.

DEDICATION

To Harry Gerecke - a fine Soldier, a caring and compassionate Officer, and an excellent friend. Your example inspires me to always serve troops.

"To the Regiment - damned few of us left!"

INTRODUCTION

Dear Soldier,

So, we don't know each other. I only know that you have picked up this book and, for the moment, you're reading it. I appreciate that; talking about PTSD is my thing. After my third deployment, I was definitely not okay and nobody knew how to help me – my Chain of Command, my doctors, my family, or me. I worked hard to get better, and I made lots of mistakes along the way. Eventually, I got my master's degree in mental health counseling and I started teaching troops. I am convinced that when we know the no-shit facts about PTSD we make more informed choices and get better faster.

I am going to write this book directly to you, as if you were sitting in my class. My classes can feel uncomfortable; PTSD is an unpleasant topic and people don't like to talk about it. I get that, but that's not good for us. Your life is at stake, my friend, and I'm not going to fuck around. I intend to be as straightforward as I know how to because I know that PTSD can kill you. We're going to talk about suicide, war crimes, depression, relationships, and more.

See, I'm one of those therapists who came to the profession later in life, and I'm not here to waste time. I'm going to teach you everything I wish I knew when I started my own journey, and, while you're not going to like it, it's what you probably need to hear.

I know PTSD is an ass-kicker, and I realize you may not be up to reading a book. But maybe you could try this one. I'll keep it short.

Another reason I wrote this book is that many Service Members know they have PTSD, but don't know what to do about it. Maybe we believe lies, like, "PTSD never goes away" and continue to feel hopeless. This book might find its way into the hands of someone who never knew help was there, and it may show them where to find it.

One last thing: I swear. I want to say that up front because a lot of folks are uncomfortable with coarse language. That's completely okay and I respect it; this is not the right book for you.

I don't swear because I'm trying to be cool or provocative, and I'm not trying to hurt your feelings or make you feel sad on the inside. Not swearing is inauthentic for me, and because nothing less than your life is at stake, I won't apologize for what I have to say.

There are a lot of great guides out there for civilians and clinicians, but this book is for Service Members. It's from one Soldier to another - from me to you - because if someone had given me this book back in 2005 it would have saved me years of bullshit.

Yours Sincerely,
Virginia Cruse

TABLE OF CONTENTS

CHAPTER 1

PTSD: What it Is and What it's Not

Rumors that are absolutely not true and just fuck with your head

There is a lot of information out there about PTSD, but it's not very user friendly. It is written by clinicians for clinicians using psychobabble that doesn't really help anyone. That's why the rumor mill about PTSD is so powerful.

Before getting into the down and dirty facts on PTSD, it's important that we discuss what PTSD is _not_ right off the bat. Why? Because *"knowing is half the battle!"*

These untruths will fuck with your head and keep you from getting the treatment you deserve.

THE SKINNY

POST means "after."

TRAUMA is exposure to death, serious injury, or sexual violence. Trauma happens to you; it's not something wrong with you.

STRESS is your body's psychological and physical reaction to danger.

DISORDER is a clinical word that means your symptoms are getting in the way of your walking, talking everyday life - that's all.

It doesn't mean you're FUBAR.

I compiled this list of untruths: (1) from folks with PTSD, and (2) from actual masters and doctoral level clinicians whose job is to treat Service Members with PTSD. So, if you heard one of these and believed it was true, you're in good company.

Rumor 1:
"PTSD has no Treatment"

Add to this: "I'll always have PTSD," "I'll never get better," and "The symptoms may go away, but the PTSD will always be there." These are powerful beliefs so widely held that many folks give up before getting started.

There are three Evidence-Based Treatments (EBTs) for PTSD that are approved by the VA:

- Prolonged Exposure Therapy
- Cognitive Processing Therapy
- Eye-Movement Desensitization and Reprocessing Therapy

They've all been proven to work for most people, and we are going to go into them in depth in chapter five.

Using an EBT for PTSD is important because EBTs are based on peer-reviewed scientific evidence. Researchers conduct rigorous studies using scientific methods, document their research in peer-reviewed scientific journals, and then other researchers conduct additional scientific studies to see if the treatment is, in fact, successful. It's a lot like how drugs are tested by the FDA - double-blind randomized trials over a very long period of time with lots of scrutiny. When a therapy method is recognized as an EBT, it's a big deal.

There are folks who are labeled as "treatment-resistant," meaning that these three types of EBTs haven't worked for them, but researchers have found alternative treatments for them, like the use of Ketamine, MDMA-assisted psychotherapy, and faith-based treatments.

Tons of money has been thrown at PTSD research, and it's paying off in spades. (Shout-out to researchers and clinicians at the University of Texas Health Science Center's STRONG STAR Initiative in San Antonio, Texas. They are on the cutting edge of this work.)

The bottom line is that EBTs work most of the time for most people. It doesn't matter how you feel; that's science. But hear this: nothing and no one can convince you something is true if you very strongly believe it is not. That's science, too.

Salient Anecdote

A few years back, I worked on a clinical team that served treatment-resistant clients. There was an active duty female client, late 30s, who had tried all three different evidence-based treatments for PTSD but was still highly suicidal and depressed. Her PTSD was truly debilitating, and she was getting MEDboarded against her wishes.

Her medical chart didn't make sense to me. She was highly intelligent, and she worked harder than her peers. Still, her symptoms never reduced to the point where she could function. I asked her what you'll come to know as "The Big Two Questions."

I asked, "Do you believe it's possible that you can get help for your PTSD and recover to the point where you'll be able to function better?" She calmly and clearly responded, "No. I know that's not possible." I asked her why she believed this, and she explained to me that, after she was first diagnosed by her psychiatrist on base, the psychiatrist told her that there is no cure for PTSD. She explained, "I know that treatment may help me a little, but eventually I'll just end up killing myself."

I'm pretty sure I shat myself. We talked for a long time about PTSD, focusing on the facts and rumors, and then she engaged in treatment with this new knowledge. Four weeks later, her symptoms reduced to the point where she could function again, and her life was never the same.

Rumor 2:
PTSD is only for military/combat/trigger pullers or "I don't 'deserve' to have PTSD"

Many civilians believe that only military members can suffer from PTSD. Within the ranks, many Service Members believe that only ops folks can have PTSD.

Things I hear a lot:

- I can't have PTSD because I never left the FOB
- I can't have PTSD because I never fired my weapon
- I can't have PTSD because my convoy never got schwacked

That's not a thing; that is fundamentally not how PTSD works. We'll talk about this more in the next chapter but suffice it to say that your brain and body reacts the same way every time your convoy leaves the wire, whether you get schwacked or not.

You don't have to be a trigger-pulling, pipe-hitting mother-fucker for PTSD to whoop your ass.

Then there's the idea that PTSD is reserved for those who have "earned it."

This often sounds like:

- I don't deserve to have PTSD
- At least I came home in one piece
- At least my kids still have a father
- My trauma wasn't combat-related

Let's have some real talk: I don't *deserve* to have the flu. I'm a really nice person and hella good looking. But flu doesn't give a shit about that. No one *deserves* to have malaria or HIV or schizophrenia, but we don't get a choice. PTSD is same-same.

> **CTJ (Come to Jesus)**
>
> When working with survivors of domestic violence, I never hear anyone say, "You think you had it bad? I went to the hospital three times!" I never hear one-upsmanship among survivors of other kinds of trauma - because it is sincerely fucked up to engage in this kind of comparison.
>
> Saying, "my trauma is more traumatic than your trauma" is unhelpful, and I hear this often among military clients. "I went to *Iraq* and *Afghanistan*," or "I got blown up twice!"
>
> Trauma comparison is shitty, and you're a shitty person if you do it. It keeps others from getting the help they deserve. So, stop it.

Cognitive Processing Therapy One of the EBTs for PTSD, focuses on "stuck points," or belief systems that keep us from getting better.

While working with individual clients and groups doing CPT, I've heard many variations of, "I don't deserve to have PTSD," such as:

- I don't deserve to have PTSD because I froze/didn't fight back
- I don't deserve to have PTSD because I was a child when my trauma happened
- I don't deserve PTSD because I could have done something to prevent/stop it

My friend, hear this: **no one deserves to have PTSD**, and we absolutely can come back from this.

Treatment takes hard work, but it's also not forever.

Rumor 3:
People with PTSD just aren't resilient

<u>In 2009</u>, Army Chief of Staff General Casey asked the head of the American Psychological Association, Dr. Martin Seligman, how to address the problems of suicide and PTSD in the Army.

Seligman's answer was Comprehensive Soldier Fitness (CSF) training, a program to build resilience and create an Army that was both psychologically and physically fit. Unfortunately, CSF was not the panacea everyone had hoped and researchers challenged the empirical evidence as <u>questionable</u>.

Still, my military clients and their Chains of Command consistently report to me their widely held belief that if someone has PTSD, it's because *they are not resilient enough -* that there is something fundamentally wrong with a troop who can't bounce back. This was not the message of CSF, but here we are.

Now that we know what PTSD is <u>not</u>, let's get down to brass tacks. Read on.

CHAPTER 2

PTSD: Down and Dirty Facts

> *Fact: there is only one way to get an official PTSD diagnosis, and that's with a licensed clinician who knows their DSM-5.*

The *Diagnostic and Statistical Manual, Fifth Edition*, is a big purple book that should be on our therapist's bookshelf with the title *DSM-5* on the spine.

The fifth edition came out in 2013, and this is important for us to know in case we got a diagnosis before 2013. **The clinical definition of PTSD changed _significantly_ from version four to version five.** If you see the gray DSM-IV or DSM-IV TR on your therapist's shelf: RUN. That is some amateur-hour shit.

The DSM-5 is <u>the</u> authoritative guide to the diagnosis of all mental disorders. It contains descriptions, symptoms, and criteria for diagnosis. I am stomping my foot for a reason: if I had a nickel for every client I've seen who said their base psych didn't diagnose them with PTSD because they did not score high enough on a "test," I'd have three or four bucks. There is no "PTSD test," we have to have a no-kidding, come-to-Jesus sit-down with a mental health professional. It takes time and effort. We have to choose to be radically authentic with the clinician, and the clinician has to know their DSM-5. Hence, there are *a lot* of misdiagnoses out there.

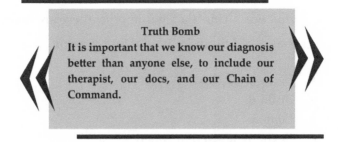

Truth Bomb
It is important that we know our diagnosis better than anyone else, to include our therapist, our docs, and our Chain of Command.

The DSM is written by clinicians for clinicians. It has a lot of jargon and can be hard to understand. To explain the Down and Dirty Facts of PTSD, I'm going straight to the DSM-5 and providing a clinician-to-English translation.

When you discuss your PTSD with others, I want you to sound smart AF so that you can get the treatment you deserve and get your life back.

CRITERIA ARE THE STANDARDS ON WHICH A DIAGNOSIS IS DECIDED.

CRITERIA IS PLURAL; CRITERION IS SINGULAR.

There are five major criteria to PTSD that we need to know: A-E. F, G and H have to do with length of time, how much our PTSD is affecting us, and ruling out other factors (like drugs or other physical medical conditions).

Criterion A: Definition

This criterion gives us the DSM's definition of trauma: "actual or threatened exposure to death, serious injury, or sexual violence." This is a big umbrella; there are many life events that could fit under it - not just combat.

- Being trafficked
- Bullied
- Beaten
- Sexually abused or raped
- Natural disasters
- School/church shootings
- Genocide
- Growing up in a dangerous place

This list could go on and on. Unfortunately, trauma is a ubiquitous experience in America. The data are clear: most of us have either experienced trauma ourselves or personally known someone who has.

Let's talk about the term, *"actual or threatened exposure."* We all have a physical and psychological reaction to threats: fight, flight, or freeze (*freeze* is the red-headed stepchild of trauma, and more on that later).

Our body and brain will react the same whether the threat is *actual* or *threatened*.

For example, let's say that we go on a convoy every day outside the wire, and that, thankfully, our convoy never gets schwacked. But we're smart cookies; we listen to our S2 and pay attention to the pre-briefs, we watch TV, and we know that there are a lot of convoys that <u>do</u> get schwacked. Guess what?

Our bodies and brains gear up every time we leave the wire whether we get schwacked or not - because our brain's #1 job is to keep us alive.

Our hearts beat faster to get more blood to our muscles, our eyes dilate, we start to sweat or shake, and our brains prepare us to stay alive.

"But I never got schwacked," you say, *"I don't deserve to have PTSD because I have my legs!"*

Stop it. This is not how PTSD works.

When we run to the bunker during the incoming alarm, read the casualty reports, walk back to our CHU alone in the dark, or literally dodge bullets, we are still being exposed to the threat of death, serious injury, or sexual violence.

To recap:

---

*The definition of trauma is: actual **or threatened** exposure to death, serious injury, or sexual violence.*

Easy day. Now that we know what trauma is, we go to…

Criterion B: Intrusion Symptoms

Let's say an intruder breaks into our home. They break in when we're not ready or expecting it and they try to take all our shit. That's what intrusion symptoms feel like. I'm going to go through these five intrusion symptoms and translate again from clinician-to-English so that we've got this.

> **INTRUSION SYMPTOM 1 AS WRITTEN:**
> "Recurrent, involuntary, and intrusive distressing memories of the traumatic event(s)."
>
> **TRANSLATION:**
> "We can't stop thinking about it, and it fucks with us."

Intruders come into our house when we don't want them and we have zero control over them. This is what intrusive memories do; they break into our mind when we don't want them to, they do what they want, and it happens a lot (our brain is in a bad neighborhood).

INTRUSION SYMPTOM 2 AS WRITTEN:
"Recurrent distressing dreams in which the content and/or affect of the dream are related to the traumatic event(s)."

TRANSLATION:
"Nightmares... weird dreams that can feel scary AF."

Recurrent means that they happen over and over, and distressing means that they're stressful. On TV, when someone has a nightmare or a flashback, they relive the trauma happening again exactly the way it did originally in real life, but nightmares can be uniquely terrifying in ways all their own. They can have elements of our trauma, elements of our fears, and other strong emotions.

INTRUSION SYMPTOM 3 AS WRITTEN:
"Dissociative reactions (e.g. flashbacks) in which the individual feels or acts as if the traumatic event(s) were occurring."

TRANSLATION:
"Strange feelings/experiences that remind us of the trauma, mess with our head, and make us feel crazy."

Dissociation is a 50-cent word that means *disconnection*, and PTSD can definitely make us feel disconnected from ourselves.

Sometimes, this looks like intense emotions that come out of nowhere, and we feel sad or anxious "for no reason." Sometimes, it feels like everything around us isn't real or is "off" and we can't really explain it.

Sometimes, it looks more like confusion. Unfortunately, this is normal for PTSD.

Since this topic is already uncomfortable, let's go a little deeper in the water: *hallucinations*. This is when we see, hear, smell, taste, or feel something we objectively know is not there.

Like when we smell something burning when we know there's no fire, or we taste moon dust when we're at home, or we hear gunshots, or think we see people following us.

I want to be straight with you:

I have never seen a case of PTSD without hallucinations.

Never. And we need to talk about this openly because hallucinations make us feel legit crazy in a way that other symptoms don't. Ditto for flashbacks.

When we don't know that hallucinations and flashbacks are an expected part of PTSD, we can feel like we're going crazy and very seriously consider suicide - and this makes a lot of sense.

What's a Flashback?

Like nightmares, flashbacks are nothing like what we see in the movies. Flashbacks can feel like walking, talking nightmares; they are intense episodes that happen while we're fully awake. Flashbacks strike suddenly and feel uncontrollable. They are more like a nightmare than a memory because sometimes we can't tell the difference between a flashback and reality. They're vivid and feel unbelievably real. Unlike a movie clip, in flashbacks, we can vividly see, hear, taste, and smell things. It's terrifying because it feels like the trauma is happening all over again. Those of us who experience flashbacks often feel like we're going insane. We're not; this is a known PTSD symptom.

We stop feeling like we can trust our brains and our bodies, and we can literally start becoming frightened of ourselves and our reactions.

We start asking ourselves:

"What if I hurt my family?" or
"What if I lose my shit in Walmart?"

I very much get you; it can feel like we'll never come back from this. **But we can.**

For now, just let this sink in:

Hallucinations and flashbacks are a normal part of PTSD.

Normal doesn't mean that it's okay, it just means that hallucinations and flashbacks are common and not unexpected. This is par for the course; **you are not a freak.**

Symptoms 4 and 5 are two sides of the same coin, so I'll group them together:

> **4 & 5 AS WRITTEN:**
> **"Intense or prolonged psychological distress (symptom 4) or physical distress (symptom 5) to internal or external cues."**
>
> **TRANSLATION:**
> **"Triggers mess with our physical bodies and our minds."**

We all have physical and psychological reactions to threats. This means that our bodies and our brains react. *Cues* are better described as **triggers**:

Triggers: stimuli that cause our bodies and brains to react.

Triggers can be internal (like pain) or external (like fireworks) and they can bring us right back to remembering the trauma. The smell of our attacker's cologne, a box in the middle of the road, the sound of a gunshot - these are all examples of potential triggers.

Triggers can really affect us; anything from making our hearts race to having a full-blown panic attack. Unfortunately, we don't know our triggers until we experience them. It's the worst kind of surprise.

18

Foot Stomp

For criterion B, the DSM-V states that we must have one or more of these symptoms. So, if we meet one out of five, or we won the PTSD lottery and have them all, we meet this criterion. This is a common clinical error; we do not have to have all five symptoms to meet this criterion.

Criterion C: Avoidance Symptoms

The DSM defines this as avoiding *internal things* (like memories, thoughts, or feelings) or avoiding *external things* (like people, places, and things that remind us of the trauma).

> *Those of us with PTSD will go way out of our way to avoid anything that reminds us of our trauma.*

Well, no shit. This makes a lot of sense: **why _wouldn't_ we want to dodge memories and reactions that make us feel bat-shit crazy?** This is why drug and alcohol disorders are common with PTSD: numbing the pain is easier.

Friends, we'll go way, way out of our way to avoid anything that reminds us of our trauma. While this may seem downright insane to other people, it makes total and complete sense in the context of PTSD.

Common examples are:

- Making several spins around the lot before combat parking
- Avoiding the drive-thru window because we don't want to get boxed in
- Arriving early so we can choose a seat away from the window
- Running errands at odd hours to avoid crowds
- Scoping out all the points of egress in a building

Avoidance can get complex, and we will go to extremes to avoid potential triggers. Since none of you have experienced this, here's a story from my own pages:

Salient Anecdote

So, no-shit, there I was in the Heidelberg commissary after my third trip to Iraq, and I was not okay. In the refrigerated section, I started thinking about pressurized dough. You know the one - those canned bakery products that pop open when you tear the cardboard seam (crescent rolls, biscuits, or whatever the fuck). Anyway, I started thinking about the "pop." When I was a kid, this little explosion made me jump, and now I thought, what if these all explode and I lose my hearing?

I understood that this idea was inherently crazy. I realized that, even if every single can of dough managed to explode at the same time, I would not get hurt. But I couldn't stop thinking about it, either.

On my shopping list: milk. As I approached the refrigerated section, my heart beat faster. I started shaking and sweating. I froze. A lady asked me if I was okay. "Of course I am! Thank you!"

I decided to buy boxed milk; Parmalat is popular in Europe and easy to find. In subsequent weeks, I would avoid the refrigerated section - no cheese, no eggs. Then, I started avoiding the commissary altogether because I could feel my heart start pounding when I pulled into the parking lot.

After treatment, I was able to return to the commissary refrigerated section without fearing for my life, but I still hate pop cans.

Our brain's job is (1) to keep us alive, and (2) to understand meaning. Avoidance is incredibly logical in this context, so be easy on yourself.

The Darker Side of Avoidance

Our families and close friends aren't stupid; they know something is up with us and they've probably figured out it's PTSD. And we know they know. And they know we know they know. We don't want to worry those we love the most, so we start avoiding them. It starts small, maybe spending time alone cleaning out the garage and day drinking, but the creep happens fast. Before we know it, our spouses are pissed and our kids stop asking us to come to their soccer games.

Chapters 9 and 10 are on how to talk to family, friends, and co-workers about our PTSD in a way that repairs relationships and gives us support to recover.

Criterion D:
"Negative Alteration in Cognition and Mood."

This just means, "negative changes in our thoughts and feelings." There are seven of these symptoms, and we need _two out of seven_ to meet this criterion. Let's go through them:

Symptom 1: We can't remember important parts of the trauma.

When our bodies are in fight, flight, or freeze response, our brains shift everything to survival. It's not unusual for folks with PTSD to forget big chunks of their deployments, or not to remember significant aspects of the trauma until a trigger strikes.

Symptom 2: Persistent and exaggerated negative beliefs about ourselves, other people, and the world.

In Cognitive Processing Therapy, we call these "stuck points," and they definitely get us stuck. We start to believe extreme thoughts, like:

- No one can be trusted
- I'll never get better
- This world is fucked

Symptom 3: Persistent and distorted thoughts about what caused the trauma or what happened because of the trauma.

These thoughts lead us to blame ourselves or others. Self-blame is common, even when we know our thoughts are not logical. These are thoughts like:

- I should have gone out on that convoy instead of my battle buddy
- I should have known that walking alone on the FOB was unsafe
- If I didn't freeze, I could have done something to save his life

These distorted thoughts feel 100% convincing, but we need to ask ourselves if it's possible that we're wrong. We don't have to decide one way or the other, but we do need to ask if it's *possible*. The reason we need to talk about this is because these thoughts make us want to schwack ourselves. More on this later, but for now let's leave this here:

If it's possible that we're wrong, then it's possible
schwacking ourselves isn't the right answer.

Truth Bomb: Let's Talk about Freezing

We hear about fight or flight all the time, but freeze is the red-headed step-child of trauma. All three, **fight, flight** and **freeze**, are all normal neuro-biological responses to fear, but, if we don't know this, we can feel guilty, angry, or like we "let it happen" when our bodies freeze in the face of trauma.

First, let's address the fantasy that we have a choice whether our bodies go into fight, flight, or freeze, because that's not a thing. When we're in danger, our brains kick into high gear and take over to protect our lives. We do not get a choice; in a split second our brains make the choice for us.

Think about those nature shows where lions are hunting gazelle-snacks. No gazelle is going to get its back up and whoop some lion's ass, so he's left with two choices: flight or freeze - and both are legit survival methods. The eye sees what is moving ("I'm up, they see me, I'm down") so a lion may not notice the stock-still gazelle frozen right next to him. Folks who design military training know this and go to great measures to train the freeze out of us. Live-fire exercises, rote memorization questioning techniques, fire and movement - we do this training repeatedly so that our brain jumps into habit under fire. But no one trains us how to get raped, or how to hold a buddy while they die, or how to respond when we see someone get schwacked. There is no fighting back, there is no running away; we freeze.

The self-blame that comes with freeze can be overwhelming. We can have a fantasy that, "if I didn't freeze, everything would have been different," or "if I didn't freeze, I could have fought back." I say this with love: it's possible that you're wrong. Freeze is not a choice; your brain took over and kept you alive.

Symptom 4: Persistent negative emotional state (e.g., fear, horror, anger, guilt, or shame).

We feel crappy - a lot.

Symptom 5: Diminished interest or participation in significant activities.

Relaxing and having fun can feel like a huge waste of time; it's just easier to stay home. Even things we used to enjoy don't meet the muster anymore: going out with friends, having sex - even low speed shit, like playing video games or masturbating. This can affect our family, too, because we're not spending as much time with them.

We only have so much bandwidth, my friend.

When our mind is busy combatting all those intrusion symptoms and avoiding things, it's hard to concentrate on anything else, especially relaxing or having fun.

Symptom 6: Feeling detached or estranged from others.

Feeling disconnected and alienated from other people is common. This is especially true of civilians, POGs (people other than grunts), legs, or anyone else who we feel just doesn't "get it" (looking at you, special warfare community).

Symptom 7: Persistent inability to feel positive emotions.

This one is going to hurt - but if we can't talk about it here, where can we?

Let's think of emotions as a continuum: on one side we have all our bad emotions that we don't want to feel, like sadness, guilt, or loss, in the middle are medium feelings like "meh," ambivalence, or not caring, and on the other end are good emotions we want to feel, like happiness, joy, and laughter. It looks like this:

FEELINGS I DON'T WANT TO FEEL   **FEELINGS I DO WANT TO FEEL**

SADNESS, FEAR, GUILT   RAGE, ANGER   SARCASM, "MEH," WHO CARES?   INTEREST, FASCINATION, WONDER   LOVE, JOY

Remember criterion C, avoidance? That's when we go way out of our way to avoid anything that reminds us of our trauma. This includes all the stuff we don't want to feel, like regret and sorrow. It makes sense that we want to avoid feeling crappy, and the hope is that we can avoid feeling crappy and enjoy the right side of the scale only. That makes sense, but feelings don't work that way.

See, things on this feelings continuum attenuate from both ends in equal measure. This means that when we avoid those crappy feelings on the left, we become *unable* to feel the good feelings we want on the right. It's a completely unexpected second-order effect, but that's how the brain works. We avoid the feelings on the left and the feelings from the right reduce in equal measure until our continuum looks like this:

FEELINGS I DON'T WANT TO FEEL   FEELINGS I DO WANT TO FEEL

←——————→
NUMB

We've worked to avoid the things we don't want to feel, but now we literally cannot feel joy, laughter, or happiness.

We end up in this horrible place called "numb" - and it feels frightening. Our spouse will come up to us and want to discuss something deeply upsetting - and we know they have every right to be upset - but we feel nothing. Our friends will try to talk to us about how we've been acting, and we can see they are scared for us, but it feels like we're outside of ourselves watching this whole interaction. Our kids come up to us crying, and we don't feel anything. Maybe we even think, "quit your crying, you fucking baby." *What the hell? Did I just really think that?*

We feel nothing, and we know we should feel something.

We can say, "*what is wrong with me? What kind of monster feels nothing? Maybe I really am an animal.*" We can start googling to see if we're a psychopath. (Calm down; you're not a psychopath.)

We feel numb for a while, and then we get an idea: *I'll kill myself.* Suddenly, unexpectedly, we feel *something.* It's not joy, but it's not numb. In fact, it's the first time we've felt something outside of numb for a while - the closest we've been to feeling happy in a long time. Not because suicide ever fixes things the way we think it will, but because we have an answer when we didn't have one before, and that feels amazing. We can tell ourselves: *This must be the best way - because why would I feel this way if it wasn't?*

We may start getting outside validation from people who care about us. *It's good to see you smiling again! You look like you're doing better today!* This comes from our spouse, colleagues, and friends, and then we start believing even more that our idea must be a good one.

Fast forward: it's not.

FEELINGS ARE NOT FACTS.

We're going to have some real talk about suicide in a future chapter because no one talks about it and we need to. I am not trying to read you. I've experienced this myself and I've literally heard this thousands of times with clients.

(If you haven't experienced this, awesome for you - you won the game of life.)

If you're feeling this way right now, put this book down and read <u>Suicide: The Forever Decision</u> by Paul G. Quinnett, PhD. It's available on Amazon for free in Kindle format and there are several places to download the PDF for free. Dr. Quinnett is brilliant, and I highly recommend it. It saved my life and I don't care if you know that.

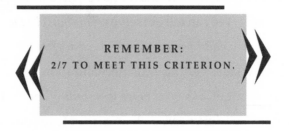

REMEMBER:
2/7 TO MEET THIS CRITERION.

I know this is exhausting. Last one:

Criterion E: Significant Changes in Arousal or Reactivity Associated with the Trauma

This kind of arousal doesn't have to do with sex. In this case, arousal means that your brain and your body are alert, awake, and ready. This makes a lot of sense because:

---

*If our brain doesn't feel safe, it will keep us on high
alert so we don't get schwacked.*

Pure logic from our brain's perspective, but this doesn't work well in everyday life. Like criterion D, **this requires two symptoms**, not all of them.

Symptom 1: Irritable Behavior or Angry Outbursts (with little or no provocation) - can be verbal or physical.

You're a Warrior and you've been through some shit. This happens.

Symptom 2: Reckless or Self-Destructive Behavior.

For those of us still on active duty, this often shows up as drug use; we know we have piss tests every time we turn around and there's a high likelihood we'll get caught. High risk behavior for troops is not uncommon in real life, but high-risk behavior on PTSD is a different animal. Think driving your motorcycle without a helmet, while high, to pick up your daughter from daycare (true case). Think back to avoidance, too - we destroy our good marriages, eviscerate our best friends, and show up piss drunk to family reunions. Total self-destruction - now you know why.

Symptom 3: Hypervigilance.

This is heightened alertness and behavior aimed at keeping us safe. We stay on guard, even when we logically know we're okay. Our brain and body stay alert and ready for fight, flight, or freeze. It's exhausting to maintain this for a prolonged period, and we can't relax.

Symptom 4: Exaggerated Startle Response.

Being startled (shocked, surprised) is an unconscious defensive response to sudden noises or perceived threats. We always feel on edge.

Symptom 5: Problems with Concentration.

We only have so much bandwidth, so when our mind is busy with intrusion symptoms and avoidance, it's hard to concentrate on anything else.

Symptom 6: Problems Sleeping. These can be problems falling asleep, staying asleep, or experiencing restless sleep.

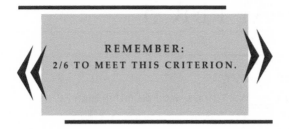

REMEMBER:
2/6 TO MEET THIS CRITERION.

We'll cover the last three criteria in brief because they are not complicated.

Criterion F says that these symptoms have had to been around for more than one month. **Criterion G** wants to ensure that these symptoms are problematic and are affect-ing our everyday real life. **Criterion H** reminds us that if these symptoms are the result of a substance (like a medica-tion) or a physical illness, then it's not PTSD.

CHAPTER 3

Moral Injury:
Combat Loss, War Crimes, and Leadership Betrayal

Before we talk about PTSD treatment, there is one more thing we have to cover together: Moral Injury. When I first came upon research on Moral Injury by Brett Litz and his team, I was floored. I thought, *how is it that no one is talking about this?* That included other psychotherapists like me.

While Moral Injury is not a diagnosis we can find in the DSM-5, like PTSD, I believe it's important for us to discuss the facts so we make more informed choices and get better faster.

PTSD is rooted in fear; our brain performs mental acrobatics in order to keep us alive. But Moral Injury feels even more nefarious because it is rooted in shame; it stems from events that violated our own deeply rooted expectations of ourselves and others. Moral Injury is born in the "should" - how someone "should be" treated or how things "should work" - in war and in life.

These are the things we did or didn't do; the things other people did or didn't do - the things we can't unfuck.

Research on Moral Injury tidily puts these into three categories:

- **Combat loss**
- **Perpetration**
- **Leadership betrayal**

PTSD is the loss of safety, and
Moral Injury is the loss of trust.

Trust in ourselves, in others, in the mission, and even in the military. And when we lose trust, you may as well take away everything else.

The slick-sleeve commander who takes unnecessary trips outside the wire to ensure his CAB. The dancing boys we heard being raped by war lords - on our base - and we were told to stand down because, "it's their culture." The beheading videos we were forced to watch so that we could, "understand what's at stake" when questioning detainees. Seeing our buddy's widow at the redeployment ceremony, the interrogations we facilitated, the beatings we got and gave, dead kids, dead dogs, and *Jesus-fucking-Christ that guy got picked up for Colonel?* Moral Injury covers it all and more; the literature reads as if a researcher got piss drunk with every single one of us after redeployment and took really good notes.

Definitions

Moral Injury can occur as a result of experiences in which we (the Service Member) or someone close to us, violated our moral code. Some <u>researchers</u> call these "transgressive acts": experiences that violate (or transgress) acceptable boundaries of behavior. When our war experiences challenge our fundamental core values, it eats away at us. Slowly.

As for why, this starts off with who we were before we joined. It takes a certain type of person to commit to the military; we call it "the service" for a reason.

Most of us were obscenely young and inexperienced in life when we joined. When we started out, we wanted to help people, make a difference, all that. Plenty of us were post-9/11 enlistees and signed up after the World Trade Center attacks. We made a commitment, to the military and to each other, and there was something simple and pure about that. *Never leave a buddy behind. Follow the Rules of Engagement. Bring everyone home.*

But that didn't always happen. We used deadly force, gave orders, and followed orders; it was neither simple nor pure.

Whether we perpetrated it, witnessed it, or failed to prevent it, things happen in war that make us question who we are now and who we can be going forward.

Moral Injury is soul damage, and, because we often can't talk about what happened (maybe because of an NDA, or a pact, or because it is prosecutable), we resort to punishing ourselves.

Litz et al.'s research found that we punish ourselves by sabotaging our own well-being; what they called, "self-handicapping." This includes social withdrawal, substance use, and self-condemnation.

We can't talk about it, so we isolate. We stuff our feelings down, jump into a bottle, and become our own most vicious critic. The self-talk is debilitating: *only a monster would ___ and only an animal would ___ and it should have been me.* We fill in that blank and play it over and over in our minds.

In describing the difference between guilt and shame, Brené Brown notes that guilt is, "I did something wrong" and shame is, "I *am* something wrong."

> *Moral Injury is shame; the idea that there is some-thing morally and fundamentally wrong <u>with us</u>.*

If the idea of a wounded soul is a little too touchy-feely, think of Moral Injury as a full-out existential crisis; one in which we ask the question: *what is the meaning of my existence?* It is deep, spiritual muck that cuts to the core of our identity, our morality, and our relationships - with ourselves, our family (especially our children), and humanity at large.

Sometimes Moral Injury co-exists with PTSD, but it is not same-same. This means that if we have both, but only get treated for PTSD, the Moral Injury can remain and continue to kick our ass until it is separately addressed. **With Moral Injury, the trauma *and its meaning* need to be processed.** We need to stare into the belly of the beast and process betrayal, anger, self-loathing, and the desire to self-harm.

3 Categories of Moral Injury

Combat Loss.
We make unique bonds when we deploy together, and we can feel personally responsible for the safety of everyone in

the unit. When someone dies in theater, it feels like a failure. There is seldom a chance to mourn because the mission must go on, and we have to swallow our feelings of failure (no matter how the death occurred).

It's hard to square conflicting feelings. We use words like "hero" and "sacrifice," but what does that mean when our brother is dead and not coming back? We question the value of the mission, the corruption of our leadership, or whether it really had to go down that way. Even thinking this way can make us feel as if we are dishonoring our battle buddy, so we swallow it instead.

Perpetration.

This is the "war crimes" section, and it's uncomfortable. This includes committing a war crime by actively participating in one (an act of commission) or committing a war crime by not doing something to stop one (an act of omission). Before you guffaw and ride away on your high horse, I want to state that perpetration is a big umbrella and it's hardly simple. It includes what we believe we did, what we believe we didn't do, or what we believe we "should have known" would happen. Notice that word: "believe." Moral Injury fucks with our fundamental belief systems, and perpetration is complicated.

It includes, but is not limited to: accidental or intentional killing of non-combatants; torture, revenge, or sadistic killing; indiscriminate aggression; sexual assault; and failure (either real or perceived) to prevent the death of Service Members or civilians.

On Killing by Lt. Col. Dave Grossman is a classic text because it does a good job of explaining how our training helps us to overcome our instinct not to kill other human beings. You'll be glad you read it. Suffice it to say that things happen downrange that are hard to square when we come home. It becomes hard to distinguish who we are in war and who we are when not in war, and we can wonder if our lives can have value when we did something wrong in the past.

Leadership Betrayal.

Everyone makes mistakes; that's a given. Acts that fall into this category of "leadership betrayal" are behaviors that are especially capricious, risky, and entail wholly unfair treatment. The consequences can be horrific because toxic leaders thrive in chaotic situations with little oversight, like war. In situations of leadership betrayal, "leaders" violate all reasonable expectations of moral and ethical conduct, and it is highly unlikely there will be justice because that is not how the military works. Harassment, hazing, unlawful orders, and sexual assault tend to be more in check the closer we are to the flagpole; but, in the field, it is game-on for venal, slick-sleeve psychopaths who literally wield the power of life and death.

Not that I'm bitter.

Napoleon famously said, "It is amazing what a man will do for a piece of colored ribbon," - or a CAB, a Bronze Star, or any other medal for that matter. Examples of leadership betrayal include, but are hardly limited to:

- Unnecessarily risking the safety of troops
- Alienating a single troop to the point where they commit suicide
- Threatening troops with violence

I think we can safely reference Sutton's Dirty Dozen here as well: insults, violations of personal space, unsolicited touching, threats, sarcasm, flames, humiliation, shaming, interruptions, backbiting, glaring, and snubbing.

Unfortunately, being an asshole is not a violation of military regulation. It's unjust, often fully known, and there isn't a damn thing anyone in power chooses to do about it.

Chooses. To. Do. About. It.

Toxic leaders shake our trust and confidence to the core.

In combat, toxic leaders undermine unit morale, and back home, that lack of fundamental trust extends to our other relationships. We come to expect injustice, feel intense anger, and can have detailed revenge fantasies. We replay messages of shame for not having done something to prevent the behavior.

Common Manifestations of Moral Injury include:

- Self-harm
- Poor self-care
- Substance abuse
- Recklessness
- Self-defeating behaviors
- Hopelessness
- Self-loathing
- Decreased empathy
- Internal suffering
- Remorse
- Self-condemning thoughts

What's Next

It's important we take a knee and recognize that our experiences can impact our lives in the long term - emotionally, behaviorally, spiritually, and socially. PTSD and Moral Injury are ass-kickers, and the rest of this book is about how to reclaim our lives.

Now that we have the facts, we are going to shift gears and create a plan of attack. First, we'll talk about challenging fundamental belief systems. Next, we'll discuss evidence-based treatments for PTSD and Moral Injury so you can make an informed decision about what treatment is right for you. After that, we'll talk about building a support team: finding a therapist, making new friends, and talking to friends, family, and colleagues. Last, we'll talk about how healthy boundaries will protect us from relapse.

It's going to take work, but thousands of other Service Members have done this and you can, too.

CHAPTER 4

How Change Happens:
An Introduction to the "Big Two"

Here's your trigger warning: a lot of you are not going to like what I am about to say (#meanlady). But to recover from PTSD or Moral Injury, we need to start with an honest conversation about our fundamental belief systems.

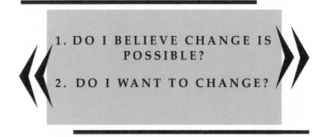

1. DO I BELIEVE CHANGE IS POSSIBLE?

2. DO I WANT TO CHANGE?

These are the Big Two questions we need to ask (and answer) in a brutally honest way before we start this journey.

Let's start with Q1.
We need to ask ourselves, "do I believe that it is possible that I can recover from my PTSD symptoms and reclaim my life?" We know that's what we want, but this is a very different question. We must ask, "do I believe that this is possible for me?"

We can expand on this:

- Is it possible that I could get to a point where I am not thinking about this every single day?
- Do I believe that it's possible for me not to feel suicidal anymore?
- Is it possible that I'm a fundamentally good person and that this PTSD is tricking me into believing I'm not?
- Is it possible that I can learn to understand myself and maybe even forgive myself?
- Do I believe any of this is even possible?

I realize that these questions are not easy to answer. You may be yelling back at me right now, *"but, Virginia - you don't understand what I've done, where I've been, how it happened - you don't get it."* You're right; I haven't walked your walk. What I'm asking you to do is have a brutally honest talk with yourself and ask, "Do I believe that change is possible for me?"

Q2 is harder because we have to ask and answer:

- Do I want to recover from PTSD, and am I willing to do the work that it's going to take?
- Do I want it badly enough to get out of my comfort zone and do something difficult and draining because that's what it will take to get better?

Choosing to go through PTSD treatment involves risk since successful PTSD treatment requires working with another person - a licensed treatment professional - and choosing to be authentic with them. I do not deny that this is hard work and that there is fear in exposing our truth to another person; we may feel fear of judgment or fear of reliving the trauma.

PTSD treatment affects our lives and our relationships with ourselves and others. Not everyone is comfortable with being wrong, and we may discover in treatment that we have been unfair to ourselves or made assumptions that were not correct. We may need to make amends, or we may need to forgive.

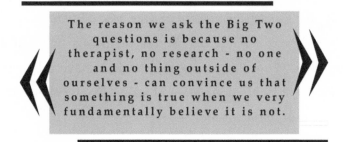

The reason we ask the Big Two questions is because no therapist, no research - no one and no thing outside of ourselves - can convince us that something is true when we very fundamentally believe it is not.

Read that text box again and read it out loud because this is a hard truth. If we do not believe change is possible, we are right. If we don't want to change, we are wasting our time.

There are a lot of reasons why Service Members go to therapy even if they answer "no" to the Big Two questions. Maybe we promised a spouse, or got Command-directed, or it was part of our probation. Not everyone who has PTSD or Moral Injury believes change is possible, and not everyone wants to change. *And that is okay.* I have zero judgement because I get it.

Maybe you're a spouse or a friend or a fellow Service Member reading this book because you want to help someone you care about, and the idea of your loved one not getting help is not okay with you.

Here's the thing: Yes, it is okay, and I recommend you stand down for your own sanity. This is hard to hear, so I say this with love: *you have no control over what someone else believes.* You can't make someone else want to change because that is not how life works. I know this feels unfair because you see how this is affecting your loved one - and you - and I realize this may be tearing your family or your unit apart.

> *The fact is that the only person who can change me is me, and the only person who can change you is you.*

Am I asking you to give up hope? Absolutely not. I'm asking you to recognize that **people get help when they are ready, not when we are ready**. And that's okay.

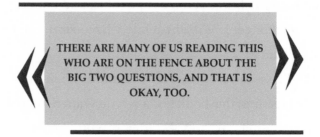

THERE ARE MANY OF US READING THIS WHO ARE ON THE FENCE ABOUT THE BIG TWO QUESTIONS, AND THAT IS OKAY, TOO.

It is 100% okay not to feel all-in.

Instead, I'll ask you this: *Is it possible that you are stronger than you think?*

Trauma warps our fundamental belief systems - beliefs about ourselves, others, and the world - and it is possible that our self-doubt is part of the PTSD.

Have you ever done something before that was hard or you felt was impossible at the time? Is it possible that your belief system might be undermining your attempts to make changes? Would you be willing to try and see if you are stronger than you think you are?

Lastly, we need to introduce the elephant in the room:

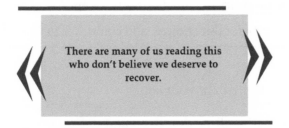

There are many of us reading this who don't believe we deserve to recover.

In counseling hundreds of Service Members, I know that this belief is not an outlier.

In the last chapter, we talked about Moral Injury, and we remember that **Moral Injury is soul damage**. We also remember that, because we often can't talk about what happened, **we can resort to punishing ourselves**.

Sometimes, this self-punishment comes in the form of choosing not to get the treatment we need to reclaim our lives. We sometimes tell ourselves that we don't deserve to have a life because of what we believe we did or didn't do. We may feel a form of survivor's guilt or tell ourselves that we don't deserve to get better because we are responsible for what happened.

So, I am going to ask you this instead: *Is it possible that you're wrong?*

My friend, if you believe that getting treatment is a cop-out or the "easy way" to do things, you need to read on and learn about evidence-based treatment methods. PTSD treatment is the very definition of taking responsibility; it requires us to stare into the belly of the beast, take full responsibility for our choices, and come face to face with our Truth.

It is Q Course for your soul.

The Truth will set you free - and maybe not in the way you expect.

I understand the existential desire to punish ourselves, but let's make sure it's for the right thing. Is it possible that you're not a war criminal, and maybe you're just an asshole? Is it possible that your Battle Buddy wouldn't want you to keep punishing yourself for what happened? Is it possible that there are second and third order effects of not getting treatment that you can't see?

This ain't my first rodeo, so here's your CTJ: it's very likely that you are not seeing your experience from an objective, third-person perspective. If you believe you don't deserve to get better, that's okay - but I challenge you to verify that by seeking the Truth. Get treatment and then make an informed decision. If you're still hopped up on punishing yourself afterwards, at least you'll be certain why.

Chapter 4

But here's the thing, friend: if you've come across one thing in this book that has surprised you so far, it's possible you're wrong about a lot of other shit, too. Remind me what you have to lose by getting treatment.

CHAPTER 5

Solutions:

Evidence-Based Treatments for PTSD and Moral Injury that Work

Opinions are like assholes: everybody has one and most of them stink. When it comes to PTSD treatment, there are lots of opinions and most have the word "just" to indicate how easy people think they are:

- You *just* need to PT more
- You *just* need to cut out gluten
- You *just* need to pray

Before you write me a strongly worded email, I am not saying that getting off your ass, cutting carbs, and getting with God is a bad idea. In fact, I don't think anyone is being malicious when they give their opinion or say what worked for them. I say, good on you - run to Jesus with your sugar-free bread! As a clinician and a researcher, I trust evidence-based treatments.

Evidence-based treatments (EBTs) are based on peer-reviewed scientific evidence. This means that researchers have conducted rigorous studies using scientific methods, documented their research in peer-reviewed publications, and then other researchers have conducted additional studies to see if the treatment is, in fact, successful. The bottom line is that a shit ton of time and research goes into EBTs and we have proof that they work.

At the time I'm writing this, there are three EBTs approved by the Department of Veterans Affairs (VA) for treatment of PTSD at this time:

- Prolonged Exposure Therapy (PE)
- Cognitive Processing Therapy (CPT)
- Eye-Movement Desensitization and Reprocessing (EMDR)

I know we have a lot of acronyms here, but the data are clear: EBTs work most of the time for most people, and they do so in 8-12 sessions.

Because these EBTs are endorsed by the VA, they tend to be widely available in Military Treatment Facilities (MTFs), VA clinics, and with therapists in private practice – so I encourage you to ask for these EBTs by name and be insistent. There is no sense in working with a therapist who is not specifically trained in how to treat PTSD; it's a waste of time and leads to even more frustration.

Researchers know that there is a certain percentage of folks whose PTSD won't respond to these three EBTs. That doesn't mean that you're beyond hope (calm down), it just means we need another avenue of approach. There is a lot of money in PTSD research, and a lot of good clinical trials and solutions to try. As of this writing, here are some of the treatments for treatment-resistant PTSD being used:

- The stellate ganglion block (sometimes called the "God Shot")
- Ketamine
- Marijuana
- Hallucinogens like MDMA
- Couples therapy
- Various treatments that help with PTSD and co-occurring disorders like depression, alcohol use, anger, anxiety, and TBIs

This list is by no means exhaustive; researchers are learning more every day, and the ones I know care deeply about all of our troops. For more alternatives, talk to an expert on PTSD and keep up on the research through projects like STRONG STAR.

For now, I'm going to assume that you have not tried any EBTs yet. Since most EBTs work for most people, I'm going to explain each of the treatments to help you make an informed decision. Therapy is not easy, but it's not forever, either.

Prolonged Exposure Therapy (PE)

<u>PE therapy</u> typically takes 8-15 sessions with a therapist; each session is 90 minutes. PE therapy goes right for the jugular of criterion C of PTSD: avoidance. Rather than avoid our trauma, we intentionally invite the most traumatic event into the session using a technique called "imaginal exposure." After learning breathing techniques to manage anxiety, we imagine and describe the traumatic event in detail with guidance from a therapist. After the imaginal exposure, we process the experience with our therapist. We audio record the session while describing the event so that we can listen to the recording between sessions; this helps us to further process our emotions and practice breathing techniques. Think of the imaginal exposure like this: it's like watching a horror movie.

When we first watch a horror movie, it scares the shit out of us because that's what horror movies do. What if we watch the horror movie back-to-back three times? It's still going to be scary, but, after the third time, we know what is coming and when and it's not as bad as the first time. What if we watch that horror movie ten times? Twenty times? A hundred times? Eventually, watching that movie doesn't affect us as much because we've seen it and we know what's coming. This is called habituation. In PE therapy, we'll be watching our horror movie literally hundreds of times – in session with our therapist and in between sessions by listening to our recordings.

The second part of PE therapy is called *in vivo exposure*, a fancy-ass term for "in real life." With our therapist, we make a list of stimuli and situations connected to our trauma, such as specific places or people, and create a plan to intentionally expose ourselves to these stimuli in a way that is gradual and safe.

I realize that for most of us the thought of retelling our experience out loud can be anxiety-provoking. It's tough, especially at the start, but PE therapy is undeniably effective. It also can be adapted into treatment for Moral Injury, which we'll talk about later in this chapter.

PE therapy isn't for everyone, and that's okay because there are three EBTs, not just one. Here's the second:

Cognitive Processing Therapy (CPT)

CPT typically takes 12 sessions with a therapist; each session is 60 minutes. CPT can be done individually or in group sessions, and it uses a workbook for written assignments.

Cognitive means that we pay attention to our thoughts and *think about what we are thinking about.*

CPT recognizes that trauma warps our fundamental belief systems - beliefs about ourselves, others, and the world - and that those warped beliefs affect our walking, talking, everyday lives.

In CPT, we learn about the relationship between thoughts and emotions and then learn to identify the automatic thoughts that maintain our PTSD symptoms.

We write an "impact statement" that details our understanding of why the traumatic event occurred and what impact it has had on our belief systems. Next, we'll use workbook exercises to identify and address unhelpful thinking patterns related to safety, trust, power and control, esteem, and intimacy. Our therapist will ask questions and work with us to recognize unhelpful thinking patterns, reframe our thoughts, reduce our symptoms, and come to a better understanding about ourselves and our relationships.

CPT forces us to get out of "auto-pilot" and start challenging our thought patterns.

Often these are thoughts we have held on to for a long time. The last EBT is:

Eye-Movement Desensitization and Reprocessing (EMDR)

Full disclosure: my knowledge of EMDR is PowerPoint deep; it's the one EBT I don't practice personally, because I have not had access to the training. The data are clear that it works.

This description is largely lifted from the good folks at the EMDR Institute, found online at www.emdr.com, and I encourage you to find a therapist who practices EMDR to give you a better description than I can provide.

EMDR is an eight-phase treatment. Eye movements are used during one part of the session. Once the therapist has determined which memory to target first, they'll ask us to hold different aspects of the traumatic event in mind and to use our eyes to track the therapist's hand as it moves back and forth across our field of vision. As this happens, we begin to process the traumatic memory.

Don't stress out about which EBT to choose; if we try one and it doesn't work, we have two more to fall back on. If we try all three and they don't work, we may have treatment-resistant PTSD and have to work with our treatment professional on another course of action.

Or, if we try all three EBTs and they don't work, it's possible we might have to work on our co-occurring disorder next. This is when we are diagnosed with two or more conditions that are occurring simultaneously. This is unbelievably common with PTSD. For example, we'll have PTSD and a substance or alcohol abuse problem at the same time, or PTSD and depression. The most common co-occurring disorders I see in Service Members with PTSD are: anxiety, depression, drug/alcohol misuse, eating disorders, and OCD. Also, lots of Moral Injury, although that is not a diagnosis we find in the DSM-5.

When PTSD shows up with a drug or alcohol use disorder, this is often called "dual diagnosis."

I realize that the idea of going through treatment for PTSD and still having to do more work is frustrating. Having more work to do doesn't mean we failed; it just means we have more work to do and that's okay.

Be easier on yourself; Rome wasn't built in a day.

Treating Moral Injury

To treat Moral Injury, we need to process the trauma and its meaning. Moral Injury brings deep spiritual distress, and we must dive into our feelings in order to come to an understanding of who we are after this experience and what it all means.

Our treatment goals are to reduce shame, modify intense thoughts, and return to a state in which we can see goodness in the world - and in ourselves. Thankfully, there are many ways to do this and researchers continue to study effective treatments.

The treatments tend to feel spiritual in nature, which may scare the shit out of you.

Ask yourself if you believe change is possible and if you really want to change, because this is going to require a no-shit, all-in, come-to-Jesus level effort to heal the soul.

Yes, it's completely worth it.

In my practice I use <u>Adaptive Disclosure</u>, which is a one-session add-on to Prolonged Exposure therapy. At the risk of sounding woo-woo, this last session involves having an imaginary dialogue with either a lost buddy or a compassionate moral authority. We discuss the meaning of the event and address other spiritual issues. I know it sounds weird, which is why I hyperlinked all the resources so you can get more info from the experts. Suffice it to say that after that one session, my clients are sincerely never the same in a good way. It's an intense experience for them, and for me, too; I find it a deeply moving and positive experience.

Many VAs offer Acceptance and Commitment Therapy (ACT), faith-based interventions, and group therapy to help with Moral Injury.

Talk to your therapist about what Moral Injury is and work together to come up with a treatment plan.

But first:

Talk to Your Therapist about Confidentiality

Since one of the categories of Moral Injury is perpetration, let's address talking to a therapist about war crimes.

I believe war crimes are much more common than we think and that we need to start talking about them, but there is a right time, a right place, and a right person.

Not every therapist is well equipped to hear your Truth.

Nidal Hassan was an Army Major and a psychiatrist who listened to Soldiers talk about war crimes after their deployments to Iraq and Afghanistan. He reported them to Army leadership and JAG in November 2009. Thirteen days later, he became the Ft. Hood shooter.

I'm not suggesting your therapist is going to go on a rampage, but I have heard a few anecdotes that give me pause when it comes to discussing war crimes with a therapist and in group therapy.

For active duty folks, our individual therapists are often military officers. This does not make them bad therapists, and it does not mean they cannot help with Moral Injury - they absolutely can - but I would caution any Service Member about talking to a military officer about a *potentially prosecutable event*. We can go to jail for war crimes.

"But, Virginia," I hear you saying, *"everything I say in session is supposed to be confidential!"*

Grow the fuck up. There is no privacy in the military and HIPAA is a joke.

Before talking with any individual therapist about a war crime, we must discuss the limits of confidentiality with them. Ask who will have access to our clinical notes, what our therapist has to report to our Command or to our health insurance, and the level of detail in the notes our therapist writes in our medical records. Furthermore, I encourage asking for a copy of our medical records and reading them. Our therapist should be transparent. If they are not, it's time to find a new therapist.

STRONG STAR, the extremely long acronym for the South Texas Research Organizational Network Guiding Studies on Trauma and Resilience, is a Multidisciplinary PTSD Research Consortium funded in part by the DoD. I recommend them as a solid place to get help because their commitment to confidentiality is stellar. Their studies are headed by the best PTSD researchers in the field and they are often recruiting study participants in San Antonio, Texas and across the U.S. Go to www.strongstar.org and click the red "get treatment" icon in the upper right-hand corner of the screen.

A Word on Support Groups and Group Therapy

When it comes to discussing war crimes in support groups, I encourage us to give it considerable thought - **and then choose not to.** Support groups are often led by paraprofessionals rather than licensed therapists, and leaders may not be well equipped to handle a disclosure.

I once worked at an in-patient hospital that had a weekly come-to-Jesus share-a-thon labeled "the war room" that was billed as a safe place Service Members could share their war experiences. After an active duty Soldier disclosed a war crime experience, another group member threatened to report the Soldier to their Chain of Command. A hot mess ensued. While no report ever occurred to my knowledge, this threat undermined the trust in the group and in the program.

I am a HUGE proponent of group therapy, and I person-ally feel it is the single best mode of psychotherapy availa-ble. Before sharing your Truth, I encourage you to (1) ensure that your group is run by an experienced group leader, preferably a Certified Group Psychotherapist, and (2) to discuss confidentiality with your therapist and with your therapy group prior to disclosing any potentially prosecutable event.

The bottom line is that we cannot guarantee confidentiality in groups because other group members are not mental health professionals required to follow the rules of ethics in order to keep a state license. Unfortunately, this makes sharing our Truth in groups a risk we must seriously consider.

NDAs and Classified Information

Many times, we believe we cannot get treatment for PTSD or Moral Injury because we signed a Non-Disclosure Agreement or the details of our mission were classified. This does not mean that we cannot process our trauma in a therapeutic setting. The key is discussing this with our therapist informing them that we are prohibited from sharing details of our experience. Next, we work together with our therapist on ways to talk around those details.

I'm not suggesting that our therapist needs to be former intel or security (although that is handy), but it is not rocket surgery to understand what is and is not classified.

Dates, places, names of units, targets, routes, and objectives are all classified. We don't have to give any of that kind of information to process our experience; we're not writing a SITREP.

We can work with our therapists to find ways to talk around details and stay accountable. In my sessions, I encourage clients to "zoom out" if I feel they are getting too detailed during sessions, and I work to ensure that we always stay in the realm of the unclassified.

If we're still active duty and are part of a special community, I recommend talking to someone in your Command that you trust; there is likely a program to help with this exact scenario. Increasingly, these kinds of units have embedded behavioral health specialists. Yes, they are often active duty officers, but they are a part of your unit for a reason (if your mental health issues keep you from going on your next trip, that will affect your team). Talk with them about confidentiality and classification concerns; they are likely experienced with this sort of thing.

CHAPTER 6

Real Talk on Suicide and Attempts

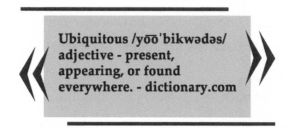

Ubiquitous /yoōˈbikwədəs/ adjective - present, appearing, or found everywhere. - dictionary.com

Suicide is ubiquitous in the military. It is likely that every Service Member reading this has lost more buddies to suicide than to combat, and it is highly likely that we personally know someone who committed suicide. We need to stop pretending that this is not a thing and have a no-shit, come-to-Jesus conversation about suicide.

I realize that this chapter may feel uncomfortable, especially if you've never been suicidal yourself. You might worry that talking about suicide will cause suicide or glorify suicide, <u>but it doesn't</u>.

First responders who go to suicide calls have gruesome tales. They know that suicides seldom end the way a person hopes, especially since most of us are high or drunk when we make the attempt. It is a violent, fucked-up way to die, and everyone who is suicidal already knows that. We *know* this, yet we still think about it.

I am going to talk about suicide in a way that acknowledges that many of us with PTSD have either tried to commit suicide or have very seriously considered it, myself included. It's uncomfortable, but because nothing less than your life is at stake, I won't apologize for what I have to say. Buckle in.

Let's go back to that feelings continuum:

We remember that things on this feelings continuum attenuate from both ends in equal measure. When we avoid those crappy feelings on the left, we become *unable* to feel the good feelings we want on the right. We end up feeling right in the middle: numb.

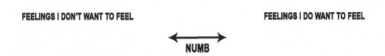

Numb is a frightening feeling. We know we should feel something, and we *actually* feel nothing. We may start to ask ourselves questions like, "what is wrong with me?" or "am I a sociopath?" Maybe we start to believe that we will never be "normal" again. We just feel nothing; no joy, no sadness – just numb.

Then we get an idea: I can end all of this by committing suicide. Suddenly we feel *something* – and this is a shock to us because we've felt nothing, absolutely nothing, for a long time. It feels *good* – not because the idea of schwacking ourselves isn't gruesome, but because we *feel something* again.

With suicide, we may not have the right answer, but we have something new. This may give us a little boost in our spirits, maybe some pep in our step. Our spouse may comment to us that we seem different or our colleagues may say, "it's good to see you smiling," and only we know why. All this external validation feels good, and we start thinking suicide may not be such a bad idea after all.

When I talk with units and surviving loved ones after a suicide, I often hear the same phrases over and over:

- They seemed to be doing so much better lately
- I saw them smiling and participating in activities
- We thought the worst was over

The suicide surprised them because they only saw what was present on the outside.

Sometimes we use thinking about suicide as a coping mechanism, or a strategy that we use in the face of stress to help us manage. We may draft the suicide letter we will write, or fantasize who will be at our memorial, or imagine the ways our family and loved ones will be "better off" once we are gone.

Here's the thing: like other coping mechanisms, it *works*. Thinking about suicide can make us feel better and reinforce our belief that suicide is a good idea, even when we know it's not. We may be telling ourselves, "I'm not going to actually do it, I just think about it." We fantasize about it more and more until we are thinking about suicide all the time. Inevitably, the stress we experience exceeds our capacity to manage it, and we begin to grasp for solutions - any solutions.

"It all happened so fast" is the number one phrase I hear from Service Members after a suicide attempt. We were likely under the influence of alcohol or drugs, and with PTSD we are **literally** not in our right minds. And it goes down fast:

- Before I knew it, I had the gun in my mouth
- Before I knew it, I was tying the noose
- Before I knew it, the bottle of pills was gone

We need to be real: fantasy can turn into action at a frightening pace. We may be telling ourselves that we'll never actually commit suicide, but it's hard to get off a moving train once we feel overwhelmed.

This is what I need you to know:

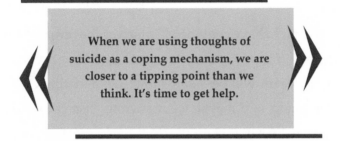

> When we are using thoughts of suicide as a coping mechanism, we are closer to a tipping point than we think. It's time to get help.

Suicide: The Forever Decision by Paul G. Quinnett is an amazing resource if you are thinking about suicide in any way. It's available for free as a PDF and on Kindle. The Military Crisis Line (1-800-273-8255) and the National Suicide Prevention Hotline (1-800-273-8255) are only a phone call away, and the Veterans Crisis Line provides confidential help through chat www.veteranscrisisline.net/get-help/chat and text at 838255.

You are not the only Service Member who has thought of suicide or made an attempt in the face of PTSD. This is hard, no bullshit, but, as Dr. Quinnett says, suicide is a forever decision.

Back in chapter 2, we learned that our PTSD symptoms can fundamentally alter our psyche and our belief systems. Given this, it is highly likely that we are not seeing things for what they are, but we are seeing everything *through the lens of PTSD.*

In other words, it is possible that we are wrong.

Yup, I said it. You could be wrong, friend. Donkey Kong wrong.

We might have convinced ourselves that everyone will be better off if we kill ourselves, and maybe we are wrong, and our death will be a shit-show. We may think we are beyond help, and maybe we are wrong because we don't know what we don't know.

I know you're tired; PTSD is exhausting. But…

You might have more grit and determination inside you than you think.

Maybe your healing will make you stronger; it might make your family stronger. Maybe - *maybe* - you're reading this for a reason.

Suicidality doesn't always look like sticking a gun in our mouths. Reckless behavior: suicide by police, mad drinking or drug use, volunteering for high-risk assignments – every mission, every convoy, every deployment. Maybe we don't need to do this anymore. Change is possible; maybe it's time.

CHAPTER 7

How Do I Find a No-Shit Expert to Help Me?

Now that we understand PTSD and the evidence-based treatments that help, we need to find someone to help us create and execute a plan of action.

I understand that many of us do not relish the idea of going to therapy (the terms "therapy" and "counseling" are largely interchangeable). We might have the idea that we'll have to lie down on a couch and talk about our mommy-issues, or maybe we think therapy is only for crazy people.

Obviously, we'd prefer to do it on our own rather than find a therapist. I get that, but there is tremendous value in not doing this alone, and instead working with a licensed mental health professional. It is valuable to get feedback from someone who can provide an objective, third-person perspective, that is 100% on our side, and sincerely wants what is best for us. Moreover, our therapist is not our friend. This is a good thing to understand because a therapist can tell us what we *need* to hear instead of what we *want* to hear.

Our therapist will not always agree with us and will often challenge our understanding, point out negative self-talk, and ask us tough questions.

The word "therapist" is a generic term for someone who conducts therapy with clients. Many mental health professionals fall into this category. If possible, I recommend finding a licensed therapist with specialized training in treating PTSD; a specialist and not a generalist.

When someone has cancer, they don't go to their family doctor for treatment; they go to an oncologist: someone who no-shit specializes in cancer. When our life is on the line, we want the best possible treatment. The same is true for mental health: therapists tend to specialize in specific treatment methods or specific client populations. For example, I focus on combat-related PTSD and Moral Injury; I'm pretty much a one-trick pony. I can do other things, but it's not what I'm best at. I have amazing colleagues who specialize in eating disorders, adolescent-issues, depression, anxiety, and all manner of mental health issues, and if you come into my office with an experience that is better addressed with one of my colleagues, I will send you to them.

Finding a therapist who specializes in PTSD and has training in an evidence-based treatment for PTSD is smart, but it isn't always easy. To find a PTSD specialist, we can get help from Military One Source, look up providers on our health insurer's website, or use our company's employee assistance program, or EAP. We can also find therapists on the internet by searching by the name of the evidence-based treatment and with our zip code (for example, "EMDR therapist Tampa 33607").

Once we find a therapist, we can call and request a phone consultation with them. Keep in mind that we may call and leave messages with several providers but only hear back from a few. (Therapists can be crappy this way.)

During the phone consult:

- Briefly explain why we are seeking therapy
- Ask what experience they have treating clients like us
- Ask if they are trained in evidence-based treatments for PTSD/Moral Injury

This may sound like, "I was in the military and experienced some bad stuff during a deployment to Afghanistan. What experience do you have helping Soldiers like me? What kind of treatment do you use for PTSD?"

If the therapist does not have training in an evidence-based treatment for PTSD, ask them if they can recommend someone who does.

Next, we'll make our first appointment. It's okay to feel nervous; in this first session we are getting to know the therapist and trying to determine if it is a relationship that will last.

It also might not be. Not all therapists are compatible with all clients, and that's okay. For example, I realize that I am not the right therapist for many clients; my personality can be blunt and my words inelegant. While this works for some clients, it clearly does not work for others. That's okay; the relationship between a client and their therapist is more important than my ego. We need to feel a sense of trust with our therapist because we have to choose to be authentic in order to improve.

Some therapists are unprofessional or simply not good at their jobs. I'm not trying to be ugly; it is what it is. If you don't click with your therapist, it's not necessarily you. Keep looking - there is excellent advice online about how to choose the best therapist.

Having a therapist we can trust is an important cornerstone for our social support network, and is vital to our recovery.

CHAPTER 8

Social Support:
The Key to Lasting Change

"Social Support." This is what mental health professionals call "friends" and researchers have shown over and again the <u>importance of social support in treating PTSD</u>. Our therapist is part of our support team, and we have to build on this foundation. Making friends is not easy, especially if we have PTSD and especially if we're male. So, let's talk about it...

Back in the day, making friends was easy. As a kid, we made friends in school or in our neighborhood, and in the military we have our unit. Making friends gets harder as we get older. I realize that for guys, it's weird to approach another dude and say, "want to hang out?" Women are different in this regard, but we also tend to isolate ourselves in the face of PTSD.

Even when we know that making friends and building networks helps us recover from PTSD, it is an anxiety-inducing idea. Some people are natural extroverts (and yay for you), but normal people worry about making new friends, especially if our PTSD has poisoned our other relationships. It's normal to worry. *"What if new people learn about my PTSD and freak out? What if I have a melt-down, or if I hurt someone on accident? Maybe I'm better off protecting the world by keeping to myself because people have their own problems and they don't need mine."*

I hear you, friend, and I want to put this into perspective. Trying to make friends is a big risk. We can be rejected, others can judge us and be shitty, and we might be really bad at making new friends – but we also know that social support is a major determining factor in our recovery from PTSD. In other words, to get better, this is a risk we *need* to take.

Because this is important, I want to take you back to the Big Two questions. (Q1) Do we believe it's possible? Do we believe it's possible that we could get out of our comfort zone, break out of that Criterion C of avoidance, and connect with another person, either in-person or virtually? Is it possible that there is another person in this world who is not crappy? Is it possible that we can use this powerful - and proven - tool of social support to fight our PTSD symptoms? Is it possible that we deserve to be loved and cared for by others? (I know this last one is hard with all that Criterion D negative self-talk rattling around our brains. I'm just asking if it's *possible*.)

Trust is hard, especially if, in our past, we've tried to connect with someone for support and they fucked us over.

Moving on to (Q2) "Do we want to change?" But rephrasing it differently. The second question can't be, "Do we want to make friends?" Because we already know the answer: NO. With PTSD we *want* to avoid other people. This is good old criterion C: avoidance. It's like asking, "do we want to go to therapy?" Big NO. So, we need to look at the bigger picture of Q2. Do we want to do the work it will take to recover from PTSD? Do we want to lessen our symptoms? Do we want the people we love *to know* that we love them? Do we want to build, and possibly rebuild, relationships?

It's okay to be on the struggle bus about this. Going to therapy and making connections is not easy when we have PTSD, but we have to do it if we are serious about getting our lives back. Let's talk about how to do this.

Different Kinds of Friends

When we think about friends, we tend to put them in two categories: (1) life-long, know everything about me, ride or die friends, and (2) acquaintances I see, maybe I work with them, and that's about it.

For the purpose of making new friends, I want to introduce a new kind of relationship into our lexicon:

The In-Between Friend:

Not a life-long ride or die friend, and not that weird guy at the office, but someone in-between.

As adults, the way we build social support is by making in-between friends. In-between friends start out just like us; they are other people who are also trying to find social support. Not every in-between friend will turn into a life-long ride or die friend; in fact, most won't - but some of them will. It's the law of averages: the more in-between friends we make, the better the chances of that friendship developing into a ride or die friendship.

I recommend that we make this our course of action for building social support. There is very little pressure when making in-between friends because the way we find them is to *intentionally go* to places where other people are trying to make in-between friends. We go with the intent of connecting with other like-minded people, and, over time, there is a likelihood that we will *regularly connect* with them.

First things first: what are places or events where people intentionally come together because they want connec-

tion? These are smaller groups (maybe 5-10 people) in which it is likely we will be individually noticed and talk to someone else because it would be hard not to. Everyone attends the group because we all have the intention to connect with others who have shared values and interests.

These are places where *individuals* come together, not couples or groups of friends. Sure, we will be the FNG the first time we visit the group, but everyone else will have had that experience also at one time. It is largely their role to engage you because they remember how awkward it was for them the first time.

Also, we are looking for groups where there is a **planned activity**. This eliminates anxiety-provoking small talk and the desire to drink or use to feel more comfortable. We don't have to talk about ourselves because we can talk about the activity, and focusing on that activity keeps us from thinking about our PTSD. There is little pressure.

Here is a non-exhaustive list of ideas for finding small groups:

- **Meetup.** Meetup is a service used to organize online groups that host in-person events for people with similar interests and has over 35 million members. Their motto is, "we are what we do," and the groups are activity based. We can look up groups in our area from the comfort and anonymity of the internet at www.meetup.com. Book clubs, hiking groups, music nerds, museum visiting groups, and pretty much anything you can think of. Their purpose is to meet people in person and spend time together sharing an activity. Fun fact: I found a photography meetup group in Paris a few years back. They even have an app for smart phones.

- **Civic groups.** These are organizations that promote civic or social interests and are often supported by a group of members. Examples are Rotary International, Shriners, Toastmasters, and Veterans groups like the American Legion or the VFW. Civic groups often support service projects and have guest speakers and networking events.

- **Professional organizations.** These groups often have networking events rather than specific activities. If shoptalk comes easier to us than feelings-talk, this is a good place to start. Google a specific profession or interest with the phrase "professional organization." Examples are the Veterans Business Network, the National Association for Women Business Owners, the Gay and Lesbian Medical Association, and the National Society of Black Engineers. Local chapters abound.

- **Places of worship.** Churches, synagogues, ashrams, mosques, and even meet up groups for atheists and agnostics are all places where people come together with a shared belief system. Many places of worship have smaller groups of 5-10 people where we can meet others for a shared activity. Examples are religious study groups, reading groups, home cell groups, choirs and creative arts groups, and community volunteer groups. Many places of worship have websites and calendars advertising their group events. If not, I recommend looking up the phone number and asking to speak with someone. Try this script: "Hi, I'm looking to learn more about your organization and was wondering if you have a small group or event during the week that I could check out to meet some new people."

- **Volunteering.** Not good with people at all? Me, either. I walk dogs at the local animal shelter and meet other folks who prefer canines to humans. Volunteering is a great way to meet people who care about the same things we do. We can volunteer to build houses for Vets or organize for social justice.

- **Support groups.** Support groups bring together people who are going through similar experiences; they are often led by paraprofessionals rather than licensed therapists and the focus is on listening and working together as a group to heal and grow. Visitors are welcome to share as little or as much as they like. Support groups can be powerful because it reminds us that we are not alone and that others have also persevered through challenges. Support groups can help us feel less isolated, especially when we can relate to others in a similar situation. NAMI.org lists support groups for mental health issues and SAMHSA.gov lists many resources for alcohol and substance use, as well as mental health and other important topics. Survivors of Loved Ones' Suicides (SOLOS) is an especially powerful peer-led support group.

- **AA, NA, AL ANON, etc.** 12-step programs are powerful in terms of providing social support and accountability, and there are anonymous groups for any number of addictions. In addition to the three most widely known programs, Codependents Anonymous (CoDA) is a powerful change agent, as are groups for Gambling and Survivors of Incest. Not everyone is a fan of the program, and I get it – there are plenty of lousy groups and crappy sponsors. There are also dynamic, inspiring groups and amazing sponsors. We can group hop until we find a group that that suits us.

- **Group therapy.** Therapy groups, unlike support groups, are led by licensed mental health professionals, and they can be powerful change agents. Full disclosure: I lead groups and regularly participate in a therapy group as a member, so I am highly biased. I strongly believe that group therapy has helped me to grow more than any single action. There are marked differences between group therapy and support groups. Therapy groups tend to be small with around eight group members and one or two group leaders. The leaders screen group members prior to members joining the group, and leaders are licensed mental health providers with group training. Group therapy is not free; it is sometimes covered by health insurance or members pay out of pocket. Groups can be online or in person (I attend group therapy online using a platform called Zoom). Group is hard work, and it's worth it.
- **Individual therapy.** You knew this was coming since I'm a therapist. In terms of social support, our therapist should be our greatest champion. They should provide us with an objective, third-person perspective and be 100% on our side. Our therapist

is a sounding board, a safe person with whom we can brainstorm, and a resource.

- **Online groups.** Full disclosure: I have not fully leapt into the 90s in terms of keeping up with social media, but I am impressed at the amount of social support my clients have found available online in chat forums and social media groups. To find one, try using a search term like "online support group PTSD."

Once we find a group we might like, we have to commit to go. The next step is to attend regularly.

Our goal is to make in-between friends with a long-term goal of building a tribe of supporters over time. Tribes come with accountability. When we miss a book club meeting, our in-between friend will call to see if we're sick; when we miss a program meeting, our sponsor will call to see if we've relapsed.

I know that with PTSD we just want to be left alone, but others checking up on us is a good thing. It is the opposite of avoidance because we are intentionally inviting others into our world, even if it's only once a week.

Building a social support network is a leap of faith. It is also evidence-based in terms of helping us recover.

Chapter 8

When we believe change is possible and we want to change, we choose to act. So, (1) pick an activity, and (2) show up and just breathe. Everyone in the group has been the FNG before; they get it.

CHAPTER 9

Talking to People Who Matter About Our PTSD:
Elevator Speech

Not everyone has earned the right to know our story, but there are probably some people in our lives who have. In this chapter, we're going to map out exactly how to talk to the people in our lives who matter - what to say and how to say it. This chapter is uncomfortable, and it should be. Our loved ones matter, and our PTSD has probably fucked up some of our most important relationships. We are going to discuss how to talk to others in a way that gives us an opportunity to recover those relationships.

I've taught this class hundreds of times over the last few years and worked with Service Members to create an "elevator speech." It's based on good science and I've seen it work time and again. We may think that our relationships are too far gone and that we are the one person who cannot make this chapter work, but we have nothing to lose and everything to gain by connecting or reconnecting with people who love us. We'll create a script, we'll choose to be uncomfortable and vulnerable, and we'll choose to roll the dice.

This chapter won't tickle, but it will very likely be effective.

"But, Virginia," you plead, *"you don't know what I've done to my relationships!"* And you're right. But I will tell you this: I haven't been genuinely surprised by anything since 2008, and I've seen this work enough times that I am writing it down. Just walk with me for a little bit.

Let's Begin

Awful things happen in our personal relationships when we have PTSD. Persistent negative beliefs about ourselves, other people, and the world takes a shotgun blast to our personal relationships. This is true even with the people who we care about, and care about us, the most: a battle buddy, parent, spouse, child, or life-long friend. We may not even realize we have PTSD when our relationships turn south.

Let's talk about the Big Ugly: we may not know we have PTSD, but we suspect something is off. We may feel like we're in a funk or not feeling like ourselves. We know that something about us is different, and not different in a good or cute way.

Our loved ones know something is off, too. They may not know exactly what is wrong, but they know something is off.

And *we know they know* something is off.

And *they know we know they know* something is off.

Our PTSD becomes the metaphorical elephant in the room.

This means that there is something in the room that is obvious - everyone knows it's there, yet no one decides to talk about it because it is too uncomfortable to do so.

Our PTSD is as obvious, distressing, and awkward as a massive elephant in a small room. We know our loved ones are worried about us, and *they know we know*. Our loved ones may not want to upset us or make us feel suicidal by talking about our symptoms, they might not know what PTSD is, or maybe they are genuinely frightened about what might happen if they upset the balance by breaking the silence. We may not bring it up because *we know* our PTSD is stressing them out - *we know* they are scared, and *we know* they don't know what to say. If we knew what to do, we would already have done it.

Rather than talk about our PTSD with the people we love the most, we choose to avoid them, and we're back to criterion C (avoidance) rearing its ugly head. It's easy for us to fall into avoidance. It often starts with the best of intentions; we may be trying to spare our loved ones from our symptoms, or we may be frightened for their safety. There are unintended second-order effects: we jump into a shame spiral and isolate ourselves from the people who love us, and can support us, the most. Maybe when we do interact with others, we get angry or frustrated or lose our shit. And we might start drawing conclusions that aren't true, like that they are better off without us.

> *Here's the stubborn thing about love:*
> *it doesn't give up easily.*

Sometimes, our loved ones reach false conclusions, too. Without information, our brain creates shit to explain why things are different. For example, we're not meeting up at the bar because crowds freak us out, but our friend thinks we're mad at them about something. Maybe we're not having sex with our spouse because PTSD fucks with libido, but our spouse thinks it must be because of the weight they put on during our last deployment and we're not attracted to them anymore. We don't go to the school play because we don't want to have a panic attack in public, and our child thinks it's because they didn't get a big enough part. We don't read a bedtime story to our child because we don't want to cry in front of them, and our child concludes, "Daddy/Mommy doesn't read to me anymore because I'm a bad boy."

I know this hurts to hear, but I'm saying this to you with love:

In the absence of an explanation from us, our loves ones will reach conclusions all on their own. It will probably be dead wrong, and it will probably become another, bigger, uglier, smellier, more awkward elephant in the room that we all choose not to discuss.

I realize that we may be reading this *after* the divorce was already finalized, or *after* we told someone we never wanted to speak with them again, or *after* the kids left for college. I get that our PTSD may have already sledge-hammered our relationships, but I want us to talk about how to invite those relationships back.

The Elevator Speech

We get the term "elevator speech" from the business world. It's brief, about 30 seconds (the time it takes to ride from the bottom to the top of a building in an elevator), and clearly and succinctly states our purpose.

> **OUR ELEVATOR SPEECH HAS 7 DISTINCT PARTS:**
>
> 1. Ask permission to speak without interruptions and wait for response
> 2. Introduce our elephant: own our emotions/lack of emotion, and let them know we're okay
> 3. Own our past - own our narrative, speak plainly
> 4. Describe our turning point - epiphany
> 5. Ask for buy-in and support; manage expectations
> 6. Love them
> 7. Silence

1. Ask permission. Before rolling out our elevator speech, it's important that we let our loved one know that we want to talk to them about something important, and we will need about 30 seconds of uninterrupted time to do it. No questions, no interjections; just 30 seconds of them listening to us with an open mind.

It's important to recognize that not everyone we love will be on board for this, and that's okay. Relationships take two people, and it is incredibly important that we choose to honor others' boundaries - because honoring someone else's boundaries is a way we show love and respect for them as a person.

We ask for permission right off the bat. It may sound like this: "Honey, I'm thankful that we have this time alone together because there is something important I'd like to talk to you about. If it's okay, I'd like to say it all at once and I promise it will only take about 30 seconds. Would it be okay if I got this all out at once - without any questions?" Then wait for a verbal yes. Only after that, proceed.

Let's say our loved one is an interrupter. That's okay. If they interrupt, just ask again, "would it be okay with you if I got this all out? I promise you that I will answer any questions you have in about 30 seconds."

What if they say no? This happens and it's okay. We let them know that if they change their mind, we are available. We reaffirm that we care about them and respect their boundaries. It may sound something like this: "I completely understand, and I respect your boundaries. If you change your mind, please know that I would value talking with you." Then, leave it alone. They will talk with you when they are ready.

2. Introduce our elephant. I'm a believer that whenever there is an elephant in the room, we are smart to introduce it. We will probably have a lot of uncomfortable feelings when we choose to talk to our loved one - nervous, emotional, or frustrated. We may feel completely numb and find it hard to connect.

All of that is okay - we'll name our feelings and let our loved one know that we are all right. It may sound like this: "I have to be honest with you, I feel really nervous talking to you right now. If I sound shaky, it's because I am, but I'll be okay." Or it may sound like, "I realize that I might sound like I'm not feeling anything right now. It's hard for me to connect, but I promise you that I want to."

3. Own our past. This is an opportunity for us to own our behavior and not make any excuses. Let's remember that this is an elevator speech, so keep it concise. I cannot stress this enough: *keep it simple.* This is not making amends, this is not talking to our therapist, so keep it short and stay on point. There will be time to go in depth, and the time is not during our elevator speech. I say again: if we are taking more than 60 seconds, we are doing it wrong.

This may sound like, "I know that since I came back from deployment, things have been off. I've been drinking too much and spending a lot of time alone." Or maybe, "I've had a really bad couple of years. My buddy killed himself, and I've struggled with feeling down. I recognize that this has affected you, too."

Nothing we are saying is a revelation; we are simply naming another elephant in the room. We are telling our loved one that we've been struggling, and that we recognize they see it, too. We don't have to go into it because they already know.

I must stress that this is _not_ the time to bring up anything new. Don't say, "I've really had a hard time these past few years... which is why I'm having an affair with your sister." Stupid hurts; don't do that. When we've got a bomb to drop, do it with a licensed marriage and family therapist present. And if you're sleeping with your sister-in-law, stop it.

4. The epiphany. An epiphany is an "a-ha!" moment. We learned something we didn't know before, we saw something we didn't notice before, or we realized something we hadn't fully grasped before - and because of this, everything has shifted. To use an Air Force term, we had a "paradigm shift" and our fundamental belief system has changed - or, for the first time, we want our fundamental belief system to change. Our Big Two has shifted: we either believe change is possible, or we want to change, and we are ready to take that next step.

It may sound like I'm being flippant here, but this is no small deal. Epiphanies come in packages large and small, but their impact is profound. What was it that made us want to change? This can sound like, "I realized after my last suicide attempt that I want to live," or, "I decided that I want to be the best Mom I can be."

5. Ask for buy-in, manage expectations. This is when the conversation shifts to the here and now. We need support from our loved one, and this is the time for us to ask for it. It is also the time for us to manage expectations: this journey is not going to be easy, but we are dedicated to trying. It may sound something like this, "I'm here and I want to change, but I also know that this won't be easy and I'll probably screw up a lot. But I believe that with your continued support I can do this." Or maybe, "Daddy has decided to get the help he needs to get better. It might take a while to see the changes in me, but I promise that I will keep trying even if I mess up at first." Coming back from PTSD is not an overnight process, and we need to let our loved ones know that we are all-in.

6. Love them. Not everyone is comfortable with those three little words, but this is our chance to break ranks. Yes, we have to say those words. Keep it simple: "the most important thing I want you to know is that I love you and I'm open to answering any questions you have."

7. Silence. This is the hardest part of the elevator speech because every part of us wants to jump to the rescue or break the awkward silence. I implore you, my friend: *shut the fuck up*. Don't go in for the hug, don't try to comfort or soothe. In this moment, we must choose to be silent.

The reason is because this is our loved ones' time to speak, and we absolutely must respect that. When we choose to be silent, it gives them an opportunity to feel whatever it is they feel without interjection and without judgment. Our silence honors their experience and it invites them to share their thoughts, feelings, and emotions with us. This is our time to be in receive mode, and, yes, it feels vulnerable and frightening. This is how we reconnect; it is an invitation for them to be with us in a radically authentic way.

Radical authenticity is scary because it means that we are evicting all the elephants and choosing to be honest, even if it's messy. In our elevator speech, we choose to be messy and honest, and, in our silence, we invite our loved one to be radically authentic with us back. Again, it will be hard to stay silent, but it is vital.

Our loved one may not be ready to talk with us at that moment, and that's okay. They may be angry, or emotional, or completely unfazed - and it's all okay. We have opened a door that is not easily shut. From here, we can let them know that if they change their mind, we are available, and we reaffirm that we care about them and respect their boundaries. "I completely understand, and I respect your boundaries. If you change your mind, please know that I would value talking with you." They will talk with you when they are ready, and, when they are ready, real connection or reconnection is possible.

Some Notes

Every elevator speech is as different as our experiences, but it is important that we **follow the outline**. I developed the elevator speech on the backs of work by Robert Rosenthal and Viktor Frankl, two greats in psychology, and this strategy has helped literally hundreds of Service Members reconnect with loved ones and forge a path to recovery.

Use notes to help. Talking to our loved ones about our PTSD is a nerve-racking experience. I encourage the use of written notes if that helps steady you - just be sure to let your loved one know you are going to use some notes to feel steady.

"But, Virginia..." **I hear you saying,** *"this all sounds pretty manipulative."*

You may be right. Here's the deal, my friend: there is no need to reinvent the wheel when we have good science and research available to us. My personal feeling is that the only way this is manipulative is if our words are inauthentic.

Place and space. It's important that we choose an appropriate time and place to speak to our loved one if we have a choice. If we're incarcerated or in the hospital our options are limited, but if we have more freedom it's smart to use it. I recommend a quiet place without interruptions.

This is an individual conversation. Maybe you have six children, including two sets of twins. Good on you, but this is not a time to load the Brady Bunch up on the couch for a family discussion. This is a one-on-one conversation. The reason is simple: our PTSD affects no two people the same and it is important that we honor each individual experience. This is especially true for children; one child may be very sensitive, and another may not care as much - and it's all okay.

You will probably cry. Not a sweet, white handkerchief cry, but a big ugly cry. Be smart: have tissue on hand so you don't snot yourself. If you don't cry, there is nothing wrong. Feeling numb is normal with PTSD and it's okay.

Keep it age appropriate. We need to use language our loved one can understand. Our elevator speech with a parent will be different than our elevator speech with a child.

Practice. I encourage us to role play our elevator speech before going live. Trying it with a therapist or a trusted friend is great, and it will encourage us. If we don't have a social support network yet, saying our elevator speech out loud in front of a mirror will help alleviate anxiety and nerves.

Write it out. Some of us have such overwhelming anxiety that the idea of talking to another person is just not in the cards for us right now. That's okay. Write your elevator speech in a letter and hand it to a loved one. It doesn't matter how we connect; it matters that we choose to connect.

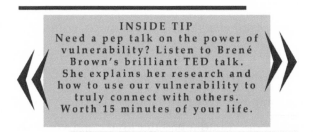

INSIDE TIP
Need a pep talk on the power of vulnerability? Listen to Brené Brown's brilliant TED talk. She explains her research and how to use our vulnerability to truly connect with others. Worth 15 minutes of your life.

Links and resources are listed in the back of the book.

Some Examples

Here are some examples of elevator speeches to help us feel confident in formulating our own. Don't worry about screwing up. What matters is that we show up and choose to be present. Yes, we will feel vulnerable. Yes, we will feel awkward. Yes, we will feel afraid - but we choose to do it anyway. Even if it goes all FUBAR, we are choosing to be brave, and that is awesome.

Example 1

Ask permission. "Honey, I'm glad we have time alone tonight because there is something important that I would like to talk about. I promise it's not bad, but it is something that I need to get out all at once if that's okay. Would it be all right with you if I took 30 seconds to get this all out at once without any questions or interruptions?" (STOP - wait for an answer.)

Introduce our elephant. "I took time to write some things down on this paper because I don't want to forget anything, and it helps me feel less nervous."

Own our past. "I've had a tough couple of years, and it's affected us both. I had a bad deployment, I've pushed you away, and my drinking has gotten worse."

Epiphany. "Recently, things got really dark for me, and I've decided that I need to get help for my PTSD."

Ask for buy-in/manage expectations. "I have some ideas for getting help, and I know it's not going to be easy. I believe that with your support I can start this fight."

Love. "I realize that I've put you through a lot. The most important thing I want you to know is that I love you, I love us, and I will do whatever it takes to make this work."

STFU. (Seriously, do whatever it takes to be silent and let your partner speak next.)

Example 2 - Age Appropriate

Ask permission. "Child, I have something important I want to talk to you about, if that's okay. You're not in any trouble, don't worry. I want to talk to you a little about what I've been going through. Would that be okay?" (STOP - wait for an answer.)

Introduce our elephant. "I realize that I am crying a little, but I'm okay. Sometimes I feel so much love for you and Mom that it fills my heart and comes out of my eyeballs, and I promise you I'm okay."

Own our past. "I know that we haven't been spending as much time together as we used to, and that's my fault. I was too embarrassed to tell you, but sometimes I feel scared in crowds. Sometimes, I get really angry unexpectedly, too, and it scares me."

Epiphany. "Even though I feel scared sometimes, I've decided that I want to be the best Daddy I can be so I am going to work to face my fears."

Ask for buy-in/manage expectations. "This means that I'll be going to see a special doctor who can help me. They are going to give me lots of homework assignments and I might seem grumpy, but that doesn't mean I'm grumpy with you. Your encouragement will really help me."

Love. "I imagine it feels scary to see me acting angry, and I imagine it feels lonely sometimes, too. The most important thing I want you to know is that I love you. You can talk to me about any feelings you have, and I will do my best to answer all of your questions."

STFU.

Example 3

Ask permission. "Mom/Dad, I'm glad we have a chance to talk, even if it's just on the phone. I know you've been worried about me, and the truth is that I've been worried about me, too. I want to tell you what I've been going through and I'll need about 30 seconds to get it all out. After that, I promise I'll answer any questions you have. Would that be okay?" (STOP - wait for an answer.)

Introduce our elephant. "It's hard for me to connect with my feelings, so while it may sound like I'm numb or like I don't feel anything, I promise you that I do and I'm okay."

Own our past. "I've had a tough time getting back to my life since my buddy's suicide last year. I stopped calling you weekly like I used to because I didn't want you to worry about me, but I realize that probably made you worry more."

Epiphany. "I've been talking to some buddies and I've decided I want to get help."

Ask for buy-in/manage expectations. "I'll be looking into getting professional help and I could use a weekly check-in again. I realize that I am the one who stopped calling you, and I am sorry I did that. I really miss talking to you every week."

Love. "I can't imagine what it was like for you not to hear from me, and I am so sorry. I want you to know that I love you, and I am so thankful you are my Mom/Dad."

STFU.

These conversations are hard, but not having social support is infinitely harder. Also, what do we really have to lose here? Nothing, and we have everything to gain by connecting or reconnecting with the people who love us.

CHAPTER 10

PTSD and Work
We Control the Narrative or the Narrative Controls Us

In the last chapter, we discussed how to talk to those people in our lives who deserve our narratives; those who support us and love us. In this chapter, we're going to talk about folks who don't. It's likely that you work with them.

Before you get offended and write me a strongly worded email, I am happy for you if you are the exception and have a workplace that feels like one big happy family. The rest of us live in Realityville with shitty bosses, catty co-workers and HR departments that are worthless. Many of us still serve either on Active Duty or in the Reserve, and that sucks too.

Here's the deal: unless we are independently wealthy, before and after we get PTSD treatment we have to go back to work.

Like our loved ones, everyone in the office knows we need help. Unlike our loved ones, they are shitty, judgy, passive-aggressive, small-talkity, single-minded asshats who take glee in seeing us fail.

But I digress.

Here's the Bottom-Line Up Front:

---

*We either control the narrative,
or the narrative controls us.*

In order to reintegrate back into the workplace after getting treatment, or in order to get support from our workplace to go out and get treatment, we have to talk to our bosses and our colleagues about our PTSD. It's not fair, and it's none of their business - I hear you. But it's life, so this chapter is going to teach us how to control our narrative, get buy-in and support from our workplace, and go back to being left alone.

Again, keep your strongly worded email in your pocket. I give exactly zero fucks about how manipulative you feel this chapter is. I am in the therapy business, not the reinventing the wheel business. There is a word for people who choose not to use available science and want to "find out on my own."

There is a Narrative, and There is an Elephant

Let's be clear: there are no secrets in the military. Yes, there "should" be HIPAA, and there "should" be confidentiality, but let's stop because those things do not exist in the military (and the civilian sector is not much different). When we have issues, especially mental health issues, *la-dee-da-dee everybody* knows about it. That's not to say that what they know is accurate, but everybody knows something is up. When we make the decision not to talk about our treatment (or need for treatment), an elephant is born.

Let me speak plainly: choosing to ignore our PTSD or avoid talking about it at work is not realistic. We can be ten types of brilliant, but all our colleagues are thinking is, "are we really not going to talk about him being in the hospital for four weeks?" or, "are we just going to pretend she never had a panic attack in the bathroom?"

We have to address it. It's not fair; suck it up. Thankfully, there is tons of good science to help us with this, so let's get started.

Science

Let's start with Harvard professor, <u>Robert Rosenthal</u>. In 1964, he conducted an experiment at an elementary school near San Francisco. He gave all the students a standardized IQ test, but put a new cover sheet on it, calling it the "Harvard Test of Inflected Acquisition." Just to be clear, *this was a lie* - it was a standard IQ test, but Rosenthal gave everyone the impression it was something new and fancy.

Rosenthal told the teachers that this fancy-dancy Harvard test had the ability to predict which kids were about to experience a dramatic growth in their IQ - special kids that were about to dramatically get smarter. Sounds impressive, right? Exactly. *Again: not true.*

After the kids took the test, Rosenthal chose kids completely at random and told their teachers that the test results predicted which kids were on the verge of an intense intellectual bloom. He told the teachers, but not the students themselves. Rosenthal's team followed the children over the next two years, and at the end of the study all students were tested again with the same IQ-test used at the beginning of the study. Something miraculous happened: the children Rosenthal labeled as "intellectual bloomers" actually did show statistically significant gains on the test.

Just one problem: these kids were picked at random. How did they experience such a shift in IQ? Rosenthal observed the students in the classroom and discovered that the teachers' expectations significantly affected the students. The teachers' moment-to-moment interactions with the children they expected to bloom differed from the students they considered "normal." Teachers gave the students they expected to succeed _more_ - more individual attention, more time to answer questions, and more affirmation and approval. "It's not magic, it's not mental telepathy," Rosenthal said. "It's very likely these thousands of different ways of treating people, in small ways, every day."

It was not the children's aptitude that gave them a statistically significant improvement in IQ; it was their narrative - it was the story their teachers believed about them.

(And it's worth noting here that no one wrote Rosenthal a strongly worded letter saying his methods were manipulative.)

Literature

Let's think about stories that inspire us. Whether fiction or non-fiction, studies of literature tell us that inspirational stories have a similar pattern. We can go all intel and graph it. We'll call our x axis "time" and our y axis "level of happiness/success."

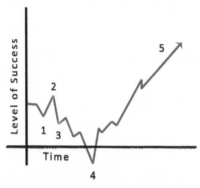

Follow the numbers on the graph and let me show you the basic structure of an inspirational story:

1. So, no shit, there I was, doing my own thing, and I failed.

2. I did what I could to get better, and it looked like it was working.

3. But I failed again. I tried and tried, and things get kept getting worse.

4. Finally, I hit "rock bottom" and everything was shit. But at rock bottom, something miraculous happened: I had an epiphany! I learned something I didn't know before, met someone I hadn't met before, did something I'd never done before, and I learned and improved!

5. Because life is life, there were ups and downs, but, in general, my life kept going up and I lived happily ever after.

Generally, this is the pattern of stories of people that inspire us. Novelists know this, every Chicken Soup for the Soul book thrives on this, and we feel inspired when we learn about people whose lives fit into this pattern, too. Rocky Balboa, Oprah, Elon Musk - everyone loves an underdog, everyone loves to see a comeback.

Narratives inspire us and they capture our imagination. In crafting our own narrative, we'd be foolish not to tap into this element of the human psyche.

Psychology

Let's look at an entire school of therapy that focuses on narrative, called Logotherapy. It was developed by Viktor Frankl, a neurologist, psychiatrist, and Auschwitz survivor. Frankl knew that personal experiences are transformed into personal stories that are given meaning and help shape a person's identity.

Frankl understood that there are a lot of things in our lives that we don't get to choose. We don't choose our family or where we grow up; children have precious little autonomy. As adults, we don't always get a choice, either; Frankl certainly did not choose to be imprisoned in a concentration camp.

But Frankl knew that man is "capable of resisting and braving even the worst conditions," and, in doing such, we can detach from situations and from ourselves. Narrative Therapy, credited to Michael White and David Epston, also seeks to externalize situations from ourselves. The idea is that we can choose an attitude about ourselves and our trauma because we survived it.

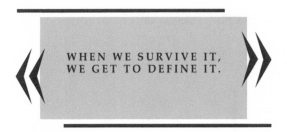

WHEN WE SURVIVE IT,
WE GET TO DEFINE IT.

I say again: when we survive it, we get to define it. We get to define our trauma, its meaning, and how it shapes us. Nobody else has the right to define our experience because this shit is not a team sport.

When we tell our story, it is action toward change because we start to look at problems in an external way; we can look at things from a more objective, third-person point of view and develop compassion for others - and even for ourselves.

Bringing it Together

Which brings us back to our original question: how can we talk to our bosses and our colleagues about our PTSD in a way that (1) controls the narrative, and (2) gets us buy-in and possible social support (even if only superficial) so that we can get the help we need?

We are going to create an elevator speech similar to the one from the last chapter. But, unlike talking with our loved ones, this elevator speech takes advantage of our love of narrative:

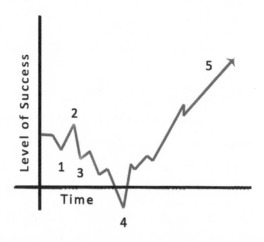

Leaning on our inspirational narrative model, this elevator speech will be tightened up to acknowledge the formality of a work setting, Court Martial, or your Chain of Command.

> **THIS ELEVATOR SPEECH FOR THE WORKPLACE HAS 6 PARTS:**
>
> 1. Thank them for the opportunity to talk
> 2. Introduce our elephant - own emotion/lack of emotion
> 3. Own our past - own our narrative, speak plainly
> 4. Turning point - epiphany
> 5. Ask for buy-in, manage expectations
> 6. Thank them, show dedication

1. Thank them for the opportunity to talk.

Just like talking with our loved ones, we need to set the stage. When talking with HR or our Chain of Command, we don't always have the luxury of asking for uninterrupted time to talk. So, we'll start by thanking them for taking the time to speak with us (even if no one had a choice).

If possible, proactively ask for an opportunity to speak with the boss or Chain of Command or HR department. This shows courage, it shows how serious we are about our own treatment and recovery, and it controls the narrative.

2. Introduce our elephant.

We remember that whenever our elephant is in the room, we will introduce it. Again, feeling nervous, emotional, frustrated, or numb is okay. Using a note card is okay, just introduce it. It may sound like this: "In order to respect your time, I took some notes to help me stay on point" or, "It is nerve-racking to speak to you about my PTSD because of the stigma, so I thank you for your patience."

3. Own our past.

This is still an opportunity for us to own our behavior and not make any excuses. Focus on work issues and speak in concise terms. Again, no new revelations. We do not have to share details of our trauma with our bosses and colleagues; keep it simple.

I encourage us to capitalize on our military experience here if we work in a civilian setting. I realize that this is uncomfortable for most of us, but military service is honorable, and civilians love to support troops (or at least act like they do). This is the time to pull out our military card. This may sound like, "When I first got back from deployment, I thought I was okay, but I started having problems and started drinking to cope. It didn't end well. I started acting out at work and got a DUI."

Notice this also: In a few short phrases, you've gone through points 1-4 in the inspirational narrative model. At point 4, you hit rock bottom. Then:

4. The epiphany.

Again, this is our "a-ha!" moment when we make the choice to change. What was it that brought us to this point? This can sound like, "After the MPs picked me up, I realized that my life had spiraled out of control and I know I need help."

5. Ask for buy-in, manage expectations.

This is why we're here: we need support from our bosses and colleagues so we can get the help we need. It is also the time for us to manage expectations: this journey is not going to be easy, and we are dedicated to trying. It may sound something like, "I want to recover from PTSD, and I know it's not easy. I'll need to attend counseling weekly and take time off from work. I believe that with your continued support I can do this."

Notice the word "continued" here. Even if they never gave a rat's ass about us, we are smart to use some sugar.

6. Thank them/show dedication.

Again, even if our bosses and colleagues treat us like crap, we serve it up in a sir-sandwich by thanking them.

When it comes to showing dedication, we get to be dedicated to whatever we want to be dedicated to; just speak plainly and get to the point: "Thank you for giving me an opportunity to talk to you today. I want you to know that I am dedicated to our team and to our mission."

We can be dedicated to getting our MEDBOARD finished so we can ETS, we can be dedicated to finishing out a drug treatment program, or dedicated to taking good care of our family.

Some Examples

Just like in the last chapter, I want to take an opportunity to give some examples of elevator speeches to help you feel confident in formulating your own. The level of formality will depend on your workplace and the personalities in your Chain of Command.

Example 1

Thank them. "Sir, thank you for giving me the opportunity to speak on my own behalf today in court."

Introduce our elephant. "Of course, I feel nervous, but I made some notes to help me stay on point in respect of the court's time."

Own our past. "After my last deployment, I made a lot of bad choices. I started drinking too much, I had problems at home, and I got into a fight."

Epiphany. "After I got arrested, my friend talked to me about PTSD and I started to see a counselor. My PTSD is no excuse for what I did, but now I understand why everything went so bad so fast."

Ask for buy-in. "My hope, your honor, is that I can continue to get help for my PTSD and my alcohol use. I wish I could go back and change everything."

Thank them/show dedication. "Sir, I thank you for your time and allowing me to speak. I want you to know that I am dedicated to my sobriety, to our mission, and to my fellow Soldiers. I deeply respect your decision. Thank you, Sir."

When talking in court or to our military Chain of Command for a punitive decision, we must be especially mindful of not appearing to use our PTSD as an excuse. Enough people have done that before us, and they were assholes.

Example 2

Thank them. "Ma'am, I'd like to thank you and our work team for giving me an opportunity to address you today."

Introduce our elephant. "I feel nervous talking to the team because I worry you may not be able to relate to my military service."

Own our past. "Since I got out of the military, adjusting to civilian life was not as easy as I thought it would be. I've had problems connecting with people at work, and I've struggled in personal ways."

Epiphany. "Recently, a buddy of mine committed suicide, and it was hard. I went to see a counselor, and I found out I have PTSD."

Ask for buy-in. "I realize that there's a lot of stigma about PTSD, and I'm lucky to have a team that is supportive. I believe that with your continued support, I can make a full recovery."

Thank them/show dedication. "Thank you for taking the time to hear me out. I want you to know that I am dedicated to this company, to this team, and to our project."

Example 3

Thank them. "Commander and First Sergeant, thank you for taking time to see me after returning from inpatient treatment."

Introduce our elephant. "I've been worried about what work would be like once I finished my treatment for PTSD, so I'm thankful for the opportunity to speak with you."

Own our past. "Before I left for treatment, I was having a hard time. I was drinking too much, I had problems at home, and I came to work intoxicated."

Epiphany. "Thankfully, the Command sent me to get help. While in treatment, I learned about PTSD and how alcohol use plays into that."

Ask for buy-in. I'm back from treatment, but I know I'm not 100% yet. I still have to go to AA and go to my mental health appointments weekly at Medical, but I know that with your support I will be able to make a full recovery."

Thank them/show dedication. "Thank you again for inviting me here. I want you to know that I am dedicated to our mission and I am dedicated to earning your trust."

The goal of an elevator speech in the workplace is to (1) control the narrative, and (2) get buy-in and possible social support from bosses and colleagues. The first will minimize drama and the second will push us forward toward recovery. It works.

CHAPTER 11

Relapse Prevention:
Setting Boundaries at Work and in Life
(Yes, Even if We're Still on Active Duty)

After we get help for our PTSD, we have to think about relapse. We tend to associate relapse with drug or alcohol use, but this simply means a period of deterioration after a period of improvement. This can happen with PTSD, depression, anxiety, or pretty much anything relating to our health (mental or physical). Relapse happens, and it's not the end of the world when it does. The key is recognizing what triggers a relapse and having a plan to get back on track if it happens.

For many Service Members, strong social support fosters recovery, and toxic relationships usher in relapse. To manage the latter, we need to talk about boundaries.

Healthy boundaries are the ultimate form of self-respect. They say to us and the world, "I deserve to be honored, respected, and valued." Boundaries denote confidence. Since confidence is often one of the casualties of PTSD, we have to relearn (or maybe learn for the first time) how to make a healthy, reasonable boundary, how to maintain it, and what to do if someone chooses to ignore it.

TRUTH BOMB: BULLYING

When we are going through a hard time, we are much more likely to be bullied.

Bullies seek out and prey on targets, aiming their venom at those they consider vulnerable or socially isolated.

Our PTSD symptoms set us up to be targets, especially criteria C (avoidance) and D (negative alterations in cognition and mood). Also, our arousal symptoms (criterion E) may have put us on the radar because of an angry outburst or reckless behavior.

Healthy boundaries curtail bullying because we stop playing the game.

If we find that we are being bullied, we can learn more about the psychology behind it so that we can (1) understand that the problem isn't us, (2) create a strong social support system, and (3) make a plan to change the situation.

The Bully at Work and *The Asshole Survival Guide* are books I recommend.

Making healthy boundaries seems like it should be easy and intuitive, but it's not. Let's start here:

Ground Rules

1. **Healthy boundaries make healthy relationships.** There is no such thing as a healthy relationship without boundaries, whether it is a marriage relationship, a friend, colleagues, or the relationship you have with your children. Healthy boundaries say, "I deserve to

be honored, respected, and valued" and this is important for any healthy interpersonal relationship.

2. **People do not know our boundaries unless we state them clearly and succinctly.** Yes, in a perfect would people "should" know how to act, but suffice it to say that not everyone is great at adulting. Some people do not know that racist comments are not okay. Some people do not understand that unsolicited touching is creepy. Let's not waste time getting mad about what "should be." Instead, let's remember that half the people we meet are below average and common sense is not common. Boundaries are not intuitive. We must state our boundaries clearly and concisely - out loud - to other people.

3. **Reasonable people respect reasonable boundaries.** The inherent problem with this is that not all people are reasonable. Sad news of the day: the world is full of psychopaths and assholes. When people choose to ignore reasonable boundaries, they are sometimes the former and usually the latter. The problem is not our boundary, it is their *choice*.

4. **Our boundaries, their choice.** We create healthy boundaries, and we have absolutely no control over other people or how they act. When we state our healthy boundaries - out loud - clearly and concisely, other people then *choose* whether they want to respect our boundaries or not.

When people choose to ignore our reasonable boundaries, they are saying in no uncertain terms, loud and clear: "I do not respect you and I do not want a relationship with you that is not on my terms." No exceptions.

The How-To

When making a healthy boundary, we want to be sure it is reasonable, clear, and direct. I suggest we use this model:

"I DON'T LIKE IT WHEN YOU ___. PLEASE STOP."

Fill in the blank. Here's some examples:

"I don't like it when you stare. Please stop."

"That word is offensive. Please don't use it."

"I don't like hugging people. Can we fist bump?"

What I like about this model is that it is not attacking the person; it addresses behavior. It is also short and to the point. We remember that this must be a reasonable boundary. We're not saying, *"I don't like it when you breathe, please stop,"* but we are making a legit, healthy boundary.

Push-Back

Let's restate: reasonable people respect reasonable boundaries. When we cross a boundary and someone lets us know, our only reasonable response is, "I'm sorry; it won't happen again." We made a mistake and now we know going forward. It's nothing personal. End of story.

Not everyone is reasonable, and we'll probably experience push-back from time to time. This will range from a surprised, "you never said anything before," to an accusatory, "no one else seems to have a problem with it," to a full out obnoxious tantrum of, "this is just who I am, and I don't have to change 'cause I don't wanna!"

Our course of action is to **simply and calmly restate our boundaries.** Here's some examples:

- "I hear you. I still find that word offensive. Please stop using it."
- "It's not personal. I just don't like hugging."
- "No one is trying to hurt your feelings or make you feel sad on the inside. Please stop."

Sometimes, the push-back gets personal and downright ugly, especially if someone feels they deserve to act however they want. Let's remember that being an asshole is their choice, and that they are choosing to say, "I don't think that you deserve to be honored, respected, or valued." The message is loud and clear, so listen.

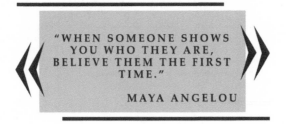

"WHEN SOMEONE SHOWS YOU WHO THEY ARE, BELIEVE THEM THE FIRST TIME."

MAYA ANGELOU

In Action

I swear a lot. Some people don't like it, especially because I have a vagina. Let's say that you are one of my students and you approach me after class and say, "I don't like it when you swear. Please stop."

You know what will happen? I'll apologize and sincerely do my earnest best to stop swearing in front of you. I may fuck up and slip, but I will sincerely try. The reason is simple: *I value my relationship with my students more than I value my need to swear.* I will choose to respect your boundary because I believe that everyone deserves to be honored, respected, and valued. End of story.

Not everyone values their relationships with us more than they value their need to violate perfectly reasonable boundaries. When this happens, we can't change the person - so we may have to change the relationship.

TRUTH BOMB: BOUNDARIES ON ACTIVE DUTY

Being bullied at work is hard, especially when we're on active duty. In addition to reading and learning more about the psychology of bullying, I encourage tracking bullying behavior using a log. Daily written logs are compelling evidence of questionable behavior, so compelling that Commanding Officers and IGs take notice. Create a spreadsheet with the following headers:

- Date/time
- Place
- Names of all persons present who acted or witnessed behavior
- Brief statement of incident, using direct quotes when at all possible

Documentation via written channels is also smart. For example, when we have a face to face meeting, we can recap the meeting in an email and send it to our supervisor and take written notes at all meetings. The goal is to have these written notes if we need them. **Having social support is vital if we are being bullied.**

But I Want to Be Liked/Loved

Not everyone will like us, and that is okay. Furthermore, not everyone who "should" love us chooses to act in a way that honors, values and respects us. When we make a boundary, others make a choice, and it is our responsibility to respect that choice - even if it means that the other person chooses to no longer be in a relationship with us. It is tempting to get caught up in the "should," as in "my parent 'should' love me," or "my spouse 'should' respect me." I urge us to collectively stop "shoulding" all over ourselves. Family members know how to push our buttons because they installed them.

Rejection hurts, but not as much as chasing the love of someone who has very clearly said that they choose not to honor, value, or respect us.

Quick List

I've introduced a lot in this chapter, so I want to wrap it up with some quick tips for creating and maintaining healthy boundaries:

1. **Give ourselves permission.** Everyone deserves to feel honored, respected, and valued - even us.
2. **Name our limits.** Take time to decide for ourselves what behavior is and is not okay.
3. **Practice self-awareness.** If someone's behavior feels creepy or uncomfortable, this is probably a boundary.
4. **Be direct.** We don't have to explain our reasons for having reasonable boundaries. Unreasonable people don't care anyway and are just being manipulative little shits.
5. **Seek support.** Social support is an important part of self-care. A therapist can be an excellent sounding board and provide good insight. So can a support group, church, and good friends.
6. **Start small.** Like any new skill, creating healthy boundaries takes practice. We can start with a small boundary that isn't too threatening and then increase to more challenging boundaries.

Learning how to create and maintain healthy boundaries will support our PTSD recovery and help us to regain confidence and self-respect.

FINAL NOTE

Since you've stuck with me until the end, I'll leave you with this piece I found at The Military Veteran Project:

A Soldier with PTSD fell into a hole and couldn't get out. A Senior NCO went by and the Soldier with PTSD called out for help. The Senior NCO yelled, told him to suck it up, dig deep, and drive on, then threw him a shovel. But the Soldier with PTSD could not suck it up and drive on so he dug the hole deeper.

A Senior Officer went by and the Soldier with PTSD called out for help. The Senior Officer told him to use the tools his Senior NCO gave him and then threw him a bucket. But the Soldier with PTSD was using the tools his Senior NCO gave him, so he dug the hole deeper and filled the bucket.

A psychiatrist walked by. The Soldier with PTSD said, "Help! I can't get out!" The psychiatrist gave him some drugs and said, "Take this. It will relieve the pain." The Soldier with PTSD said thanks, but when the pills ran out, he was still in the hole.

A well-known psychologist rode by and heard the Soldier with PTSD crying for help. He stopped and asked, "How did you get there? Were you born there? Did your parents put you there? Tell me about yourself, it will alleviate your sense of loneliness." So, the Soldier with PTSD talked with him for an hour, then the psychologist had to leave, but he said he'd be back next week. The Soldier with PTSD thanked him, but he was still in the hole.

A priest came by. The Soldier with PTSD called for help. The priest gave him a Bible and said, "I'll say a prayer for you." He got down on his knees and prayed for the Soldier with PTSD, then he left. The Soldier with PTSD was very grateful, he read the Bible, but he was still stuck in the hole.

A recovering Soldier with PTSD happened to be passing by. The Soldier with PTSD cried out, "Hey, help me. I'm stuck in this hole!" Right away the recovering Soldier with PTSD jumped down in the hole with him. The Soldier with PTSD said, "What are you doing? Now we're both stuck here!" But the recovering Soldier with PTSD said, "Calm down. It's okay. I've been here before. I know how to get out."

-Author Unknown

I wrote this book for you because I've been there before and I know how to get out. Now I want you to recover so we can jump in holes together.

We've covered a lot: what PTSD is and isn't, Moral Injury, what treatments work, how to find treatment and social support, how to talk to others about our PTSD, and how to protect our recovery through healthy boundaries.

My hope is that you have a lot more tools now than when you started.

I would be happy to hear from you and answer your questions. Ping me at ContactUs@TheSoldiersGuide.com. I'll use your feedback for future editions of this book.

Take care of yourself.

Links and Resources

The Veterans Crisis Line
www.veteranscrisisline.net/get-help/
chat Text at 838255.

Comprehensive Soldier Fitness (CSF) training
information https://hbr.org/2011/03/post-traumatic-
growth-and-buil
National Estimates of Exposure to Traumatic Events and
PTSD Prevalence Using DSM-4 and DSM-5 Criteria
https://www.ncbi.nlm.nih.gov/pmc/articles/PMC4096796/

Suicide: The Forever Decision by Paul G. Quinnett, PhD.
http://www.ryanpatrickhalligan.org/documents/
Forever_Decision._pdf

Moral Injury by Brett Litz
https://www.sciencedirect.com/science/article/pii/
S0272735809000 920?via%3Dihub

Transgressive Acts
http://dx.doi.org/10.1037/
mil0000132
In describing the difference between guilt and shame, by Brené
Brown
https://www.ted.com/talks/brene_brown_listening_to_shame?
lang uage=en

On Killing by Lt. Col. Dave Grossman
https://en.wikipedia.org/wiki/
On_Killing

Sutton's Dirty Dozen
https://www.amazon.com/dp/0446698202

STRONG STAR
http://www.strongstar.org/

EMDR Institute
www.emdr.com

Adaptive Disclosure
https://www.amazon.com/dp/1462533833/

Nidal Hassan / Confidentiality
https://www.nytimes.com/2013/08/21/us/fort-hood-gunman-nidal-malik-hasan.html

Certified Group Psychotherapist
http://member.agpa.org/imis/agpa/cgpdirectory/cgpdirectory.aspx

Does asking about suicide and related behaviours induce suicidal ideation? What is the evidence?
https://www.ncbi.nlm.nih.gov/pubmed/24998511

To find a PTSD specialist, we can get help from Military One Source
https://www.militaryonesource.mil/confidential-help

How to choose the best therapist
https://www.psychologytoday.com/us/blog/freudian-sip/201102/how-find-the-best-therapist-you

The importance of social support in treating PTSD
https://www.ncbi.nlm.nih.gov/pmc/articles/PMC5507582/

Support groups
http://www.nami.org/
http://www.samhsa.gov/
https://suicidology.org/resources/support-groups/

Harvard professor, Robert Rosenthal experiment
https://www.npr.org/sections/health-shots/2012/09/18/161159263/teachers-expectations-can-influence-how-students-perform

The Bully at Work
https://www.amazon.com/Bully-Work-What-Reclaim-Dignity/dp/1402224265

The Asshole Survival Guide
https://www.amazon.com/Asshole-Survival-Guide-Robert-Sutton/dp/1328511669/

About Prolonged Exposure Therapy
https://www.med.upenn.edu/ctsa/workshops_pet.html

About Cognitive Processing Therapy
https://cptforptsd.com/

About Eye Movement Desensitization and Reprocessing
https://www.emdr.com/what-is-emdr/

INDEX

Your opinion matters!

When people first look at a book, beyond the description and the cover, they pay close attention to what others like you have to say. Reviews heavily influence that reader's decision to make a purchase.

You don't have to write a novel—that's my job! Simply share what you thought of the book by answering two very simple questions:

• Was the information valuable?
• Would you recommend it to someone else?

That's it!

Your opinion matters. It matters to me, because I want to ensure you are getting the most accurate and helpful information. And beyond my desire to educate you, the review you write could make (or break) the success of this book.

ABOUT THE AUTHOR

Virginia Cruse is a Licensed Professional Counselor and National Certified Counselor specializing in Military Issues and Combat-Related Trauma. She provides crisis intervention and evidence-based treatments for Post-Traumatic Stress Disorder, Moral Injury, Depression, Combat Operational Stress, and other diagnoses. Virginia is a certified clinician in Cognitive Processing Therapy and Prolonged Exposure Therapy and has 20+ years' experience serving Active Duty Military, Veterans, Military retirees and family members. She is a Certified Group Psychotherapist and active American Group Psychotherapy Association member. Virginia is an Army Reserve Officer, Combat Veteran, and published researcher. She has one amazing husband, Jay, and one terrible dog, Peanut.

Virginia practices in Texas and Louisiana.

Find out more at:

www.MilitaryCounselingSA.com

Email me at:

ContactUs@TheSoldiersGuide.com

Acknowledgements

Scott Mendoza: without a doubt, I would have never finished this project if it were not for you. Thank you for your feedback, encouragement, and persistence.

Many thanks to my friends and colleagues who provided excellent feedback: Harry Gerecke, Nikita Kranda, Larry Liebgold, Brian Mazuc, Denny McCollough, Scott Mendoza, Derek Pollett, Kristyn Ray, Ted Rochford, Kathleen Salidas, and Kathy Telford.

Thank you to the researchers and treatment professionals who serve Service Members, Veterans, and their families. You are needed.

Made in United States
Troutdale, OR
07/26/2023

11586380R00094